.

David Humphreys

Twayne's United States Authors Series

Mason Lowance, Editor

University of Massachusetts, Amherst

TUSAS 428

DAVID HUMPHREYS
(1752–1818)
*Photograph of a painting by
Gilbert Stuart. Reprinted by
permission of Yale University
Art Gallery. Gift of the widow
of General Humphreys in 1830.*

David Humphreys

By Edward M. Cifelli

County College of Morris

Twayne Publishers • Boston

David Humphreys

Edward M. Cifelli

Copyright © 1982 by G. K. Hall & Company
Published by Twayne Publishers
A Division of G. K. Hall & Company
70 Lincoln Street
Boston, Massachusetts 02111

Book Production by Marne B. Sultz

Book Design by Barbara Anderson

Printed on permanent/durable acid-free
paper and bound in The United States
of America.

Library of Congress Cataloging in Publication Data

Cifelli, Edward M.
  David Humphreys.

  (Twayne's United States authors series ; TUSAS 428)
  Bibliography: p. 136
  Includes index.
  1. Humphreys, David, 1752–1818—Criticism and
interpretation.   I. Title.   II. Series.
PS778.H5Z6   818'.209   81–20257
ISBN 0–8057–7363–0   AACR2

For Bobbi

Contents

About the Author

Edward M. Cifelli received the B.A. from Rutgers University, M.A.s from Texas Tech University and New York University, and the Ph.D. in American Studies from NYU. Since 1969 he has taught American literature—among other things—at County College of Morris in northwest New Jersey, where he is an associate professor of English and coordinator of the Honors Program. Professor Cifelli has published articles on a variety of American authors, including Cotton Mather, David Humphreys, Nathaniel Hawthorne, Herman Melville, John Ciardi, and Robert Frost. He has also coedited three volumes of the annual *Index of American Periodical Verse*, for which he received a research grant from the National Endowment for the Humanities (1977).

Preface

If there is a single idea informing this volume on David Humphreys, it is that he was a multidimensional figure of the American Enlightenment and that, while not a great man, he occupies a deserved—albeit minor—position among the cosmopolitan thinkers of the eighteenth century. Humphreys was a patriot, diplomat, businessman, poet, biographer, playwright, and scientist. He was aide-de-camp to Generals Putnam, Greene, and Washington, achieving the rank of lieutenant colonel, and saw duty also during Shays' Rebellion and the War of 1812. As a diplomat, he was the United States' first Minister Resident to Portugal and Minister Plenipotentiary to Spain, and he played a significant role in the 1796 release of the Algerine captives. As a businessman from 1802–1818, he developed a flock of merino sheep, which for many years formed the nucleus of America's finest woolen industry. In addition, he wrote a popular biography of Israel Putnam, wrote and produced two plays, and was admitted to the Royal Society. Simultaneous to all these pursuits, David Humphreys was a poet of stature during his own lifetime, and, with Timothy Dwight, Joel Barlow, and John Trumbull, he was one of the four major Connecticut Wits.

This book is primarily concerned with Humphreys' literary career, which he viewed as a proper avocation for an eighteenth-century gentleman. It examines, for the first time, the direct relationship of Humphreys' poetry to the rhetorical and oratorical formulas popular in the late eighteenth century, particularly to the epideictic speech. Several attributions are made here for the first time; of particular significance are the supported conclusions drawn about the extent of Humphreys' contribution to *The Anarchiad,* long a moot point among scholars.

There have been three important commentators on David Humphreys in the twentieth century; each has made key contributions to Humphreys scholarship. First was Frank Landon Humphreys in a two-volume biography of his ancestor in 1917. Predictably, this "life and times" biography is characterized by studiousness and piety; it is filial, devotional, and openly admiring. Its greatest virtue is also its greatest defect, that is, an extraordinary—and undiscriminating—comprehensiveness. The many letters and other documents reprinted at length in both volumes constitute one of the richest sources of primary materials on Humphreys' mature life and work. Fortunately, Frank Landon Humphreys' transcriptions have proved to be reliable, a fact which takes on added significance because letters fill up approximately 75 percent of Volume II. On the other hand, this biography, despite its great size, contains very little about David Humphreys as an eighteenth-century literary figure.

The second commentator was Vernon L. Parrington, who published *The Connecticut Wits* in 1926. In this anthology Parrington said Humphreys was "perhaps the most attractive of the entire group" and that he was both likable and capable. Parrington made Humphreys available but did not examine the work closely—that was done by Leon Howard in a 1943 book, also titled *The Connecticut Wits*. This book contained two rather critical chapters on Humphreys and may be partly responsible for the slightly tarnished image of Humphreys that has since existed. Howard concluded—too hastily—that Humphreys was guilty of hero-worship and, worse, that he somehow managed to convert public poetry into personal gain.

The present study attempts a more complete and balanced view of David Humphreys as a literary figure than has yet appeared. Perhaps, as a result of this study, readers may be inclined to reread and reappraise David Humphreys' patriotic verse, for his was an interesting, minor contribution to a developing American literature. Humphreys was a prominent figure of the American Enlightenment: his rapid advancement was due to his talents, and his literary efforts were the natural expressions of a patriotic spirit. David Humphreys will be judged here by the quality of his many successes, literary and otherwise, not by his limitations.

This volume has many specific debts, too many to acknowledge individually. Among them, however, none is greater than my debt to Kenneth Silverman of New York University for leading me through the first years and providing regular encouragement there-after. I would be remiss as well if I did not thank my two research assistants, Milton Dickerson and Leonard Ingrando. Library staffs throughout the United States were uniformly helpful and are ac-knowledged later in the bibliography. To the many other profes-sionals who touched some part of this book at one time or another, please accept my apologies for not listing you individually and my thanks for your kind and generous help. I take a sincere happiness as well in thanking my students, with whom I have shared ideas and grown for the past fifteen years.

A special, heartfelt acknowledgement goes to Warren S. Walker, Horn Professor of English at Texas Tech University, who continues to be for me the perfect blend of teacher, scholar, and friend. His lessons have extended well beyond the classroom.

Most of all, happily, my thanks and gratitude go to my family: to Pat and Annette, my parents; to Edith Brunson, my mother-in-law; to Laura and Lisa, my delightfully unpredictable daughters; and to the lovely Roberta Louise, my wife—to whom this book is justly dedicated. It was only through their collective patience, good humor, and love that this book could have been written.

Edward M. Cifelli

County College of Morris

Chronology

1786	Summer: visited with the Washington family at Mount Vernon for five weeks; autumn: elected to the Connecticut Assembly.
1787	Autumn: moved permanently to Mount Vernon; wrote *The Widow of Malabar* and *Life of Putnam.*
1788	His poetry is featured in the *American Museum* (March 1788).
1789	30 April: was with Washington in New York at the inauguration; stayed on as secretary; published first collection of occasional verse, *Poems.*
1790	Published *The Miscellaneous Works of Colonel Humphreys;* sent on a diplomatic mission to Portugal and Spain; remained in Europe for all but one of the next twelve years.
1791	Named Minister Resident to the court at Lisbon.
1792	Wrote "A Poem on Industry."
1793	Commissioned by Washington to negotiate with the Dey of Algiers for the freedom of the Algerine captives.
1796	20 May: appointed America's first full Minister Plenipotentiary to the court at Madrid.
1797	8 May: married Miss Ann Frances Bulkeley.
1799	Wrote "A Poem on the Love of Country."
1800	Wrote "A Poem on the Death of General Washington."
1801	April: recalled from Spain by Thomas Jefferson.
1802	Arrived back in the United States; began woolen manufacturing industry in Connecticut with 100 merino sheep, a gift of the Spanish court.
1804	Published *The Miscellaneous Works of David Humphreys.*
1807	11 June: admitted to the Royal Society as a Fellow.
1813	Commissioned brigadier-general in Connecticut militia.

1815–1816   Published and produced *The Yankey in England,* a comedy.

1818   21 February: died of heart failure at age sixty-five; buried at the Grove Street Cemetery in New Haven.

Chapter One

Apprentice

Introduction

Despite his contemporary renown during the Revolution and the numerous public records that fill out his middle and later years, much of the early life of David Humphreys remains obscure. His father, the Reverend Daniel Humphrey[s], was, at the time of David's birth, pastor of the Congregational Church in Derby, Connecticut. His mother, the widowed Sarah Bowers, had married the Reverend Humphrey[s] in April 1739. David, born on 10 July 1752, was the youngest of their five children. The young man enrolled at Yale in 1767 and became active in school life at once. He was denied membership in the school literary society, however, because freshmen were not eligible, so he helped organize a competing society, Brothers in Unity, and thus began a career in oratory and debate that lasted through most of his adult life. Upon graduation, Humphreys became a schoolmaster at Wethersfield, Connecticut, and later still he signed on as a tutor for the younger children at the Philipse Manor in New York.

During the summer of 1776, however, Humphreys left the Loyalist Philipse family in order to fight on the side of the patriots. He joined Washington's army late in August 1776. In March 1777 Humphreys was appointed brigade-major of General Samuel Parsons' Connecticut Line. A year and a half after that, in December 1778, he joined Israel Putnam's military family as aide-de-camp. When Putnam suffered a stroke, in December 1779, Humphreys was forced into spending some five months idle. During this time he wrote a number of his best poems, including the "Address to the Armies." In May 1780, he joined Nathaniel Greene and a month after that was appointed aide-de-camp to George Washington. This was the start of their long and close friendship, which lasted until Washington's death in 1799. Throughout the remainder of the war, Humphreys was near the Commander-in-Chief, and often he figured prominently in the war effort. After Cornwallis's surrender at Yorktown, for example, it was David Humphreys who was given the responsibility and honor of riding north to turn over the surrendered British standards to Congress in Philadelphia. Humphreys remained with Washington until early 1784, when he returned home to Connecticut.

In May 1784, just when it appeared that Humphreys' public career was over, it was put in motion once again: he was invited to become secretary to a commission empowered to negotiate commercial treaties in Europe. The commissioners were John Adams, Benjamin Franklin, and Thomas Jefferson. During his nearly two years in Paris and London, Humphreys found time to write a long work entitled "A Poem on the Happiness of America" in which he attempted to show citizens of America the many ways God had singled out this new nation for special favors. The poem was extremely popular and went through some nine editions and numerous additional reprintings.

Upon his arrival back in the United States in early 1786, Humphreys visited his home and made stops in New Haven and New York before turning south to visit the Washington family at Mount Vernon. He spent five weeks there enjoying the friendship and hospitality that the family always gave him; Humphreys also at this time began an interesting but never-to-be-completed biography of Washington. In September he returned home and was elected to the Connecticut Assembly.

During the fall of 1786 Humphreys found himself angrily observing the social, economic, and military disturbances which came to be known as Shays' Rebellion. Humphreys helped counter the rebellion by taking command of a regiment of Connecticut militia, but his greater effect on the insurgents was felt through his collaboration with other so-called Connecticut Wits in a work entitled *The Anarchiad: A Poem on the Restoration of Chaos and Substantial Night,* which appeared in twelve numbers between October 1786 and September 1787. Although the individual, satiric numbers of

The Anarchiad enjoyed wide circulation through reprints in many local newspapers, their overall effect on the Constitutional Convention is hard to gauge. That they did have an impact on public opinion is, however, quite certain.

In October 1787, Humphreys accepted Washington's invitation to become a permanent member of the Mount Vernon household. While there, Humphreys translated a play, *The Widow of Malabar,* completed his well-known *Essay on the Life of the Honourable Major-General Israel Putnam,* and saw his first book of poems published. In 1790 he published the first edition of *Miscellaneous Works,* a collection of his works that had, for the most part, been previously published. Also in 1790 Washington sent Humphreys on a series of diplomatic missions that took him to London, Lisbon, and Madrid, thus launching a diplomatic career that lasted nearly twelve years.

During his time in European capitals, Humphreys' achievements were notable. For example, in 1791 he was appointed the United States' first Minister Resident to the court at Lisbon. In that position Humphreys overcame many frustrating delays and was instrumental in freeing the American hostages, held by the Dey of Algiers, in 1795–96. In recognition of Humphreys' fine work, Washington appointed Humphreys the United States' first Minister Plenipotentiary to the court at Madrid. Time and again Washington put trust in his young friend, and time and again Humphreys proved his value. From a literary standpoint it is important to note that even during the years of his important diplomatic work, Humphreys continued writing poetry. Three of his longest and most distinguished poems were written at that time: "Poem on the National Industry of the U.S." (1792), "A Poem on the Love of Country" (1799), and "A Poem on the Death of General Washington" (1800). Humphreys kept his position in Madrid during the presidency of John Adams, but Thomas Jefferson, in a flagrantly political move, recalled Humphreys. The two men, who had once been close, found themselves more and more estranged as Humphreys remained a Washington-styled Federalist and Jefferson continued to lead the new political opposition.

Humphreys and his wife, the former Ann Frances Bulkeley, whom he had married in 1797, arrived at New York from Madrid in the spring of 1802. With them were some one hundred prize merino sheep that had been given Humphreys as a special gift by the Spanish government. These were to form the nucleus of what was soon to become America's finest woolen industry. At about the same time, Humphreys was also involved with the publication of a revised edition of his *Miscellaneous Works* (published in 1804). This collection of his poems and prose is not complete, though it is nearly so; it is, nonetheless, considered the standard edition of Humphreys' works.

The last eighteen years of Humphreys' life were spent with a curious mix of personal satisfaction over his business success and political disaffection over the country's gradual movement away from Federalism and toward Jeffersonian Republicanism. His was a Federalist voice from the past, and although he was in a position to be one of America's venerable senior statesmen, a position he no doubt coveted, he was ignored. The peculiarity of his position was illustrated by the personal crisis he faced during the War of 1812. Humphreys had dedicated his life to the creation and preservation of the fragile, new nation, but he found himself unable to support the war effort against England. Humphreys "resolved" the conflict by serving, provincially, with his neighbors in the Connecticut militia to protect their own state. At the same time, he urged a speedy ceasefire and an equally speedy peace treaty.

In 1815 Humphreys produced his play, *The Yankey in England,* casting it with the young men and boys employed at his mill in Humphreysville. The comedy had been over twenty years in the making, and while it is not altogether successful as drama, it does have one notable character, the "Yankey" Doolittle, whose mannerisms and speech patterns are faithfully rendered according to type. Less than three years later, on 21 February 1818, Humphreys died unexpectedly of heart failure in New Haven.

Yale Years

David Humphreys was born into the era of the Revolution with a distinguished colonial American heritage, accounting in some measure for the ardent patriotism which most characterized him throughout his life. One of his great-grandfathers had stood with New England's first families in the mid-seventeenth century urging reforms in the strict regulations determining church membership, reforms which, when finally enacted, gradually became known as the Half Way Covenant. Another of his ancestors was a soldier, Sergeant Edward Riggs, who was one of the small group that captured the Pequot Fort in Groton in 1637, saving the settlements. Later, in the early 1660s, Riggs had the temerity to offer his home to the regicides: William Goffe, Edward Whalley, and John Dixwell.

These Colonial American roots, however, were but a single part of David Humphreys' birthright. The Reverend Daniel Humphrey[s] had bequeathed his son religious orthodoxy and a literary inclination. Equally important, he built on David's early schooling by drilling him in Latin and English grammar as well as rhetoric. In his father's library the young man encountered the works of Samuel Johnson and various volumes of the *Spectator,* matter that influenced the development of his taste for literature and belles lettres. Throughout his youth David Humphreys was surrounded by books and learning, and, by virtue of his familiarity with Cicero, Virgil, and the Greek Testaments, he was ready for admission to Yale in 1767, at age fifteen.

His ancestral roots and his father's religious orthodoxy were not the only influences of tradition on David Humphreys: Yale was another. There he adopted the Neoclassic appreciation of reason, order, moralism, and social responsibility. The course offerings at Yale in the last half of the eighteenth century were well established by tradition. Alexander Cowie has correctly observed that "disciplining the mind, not expanding or broadening it, was the ideal of contemporary education. . . . The Yale curriculum . . . had long been shaped by a conservative policy."[1] The conservative atmosphere of Yale in 1767 contributed to a much weakened but still recognizable version of the seventeenth century's idea of visible sainthood: God's chosen people were at Yale.

The importance of religious training at Yale between 1767 and 1771 is suggested by the senior year study of divinity, which every student took under the direct tutelage of the president, Naphtali Dagget. The divinity textbook, William Wollaston's *The Religion of Nature Delineated,* implied an elitism similar in its way to what Federalism would be in the 1790s. Wollaston wrote: "The reason why the *many* are so commonly in the wrong and so wretchedly misjudge things [is that] the generality of people are not sufficiently prepared, by a proper education, to find truth by reasoning."[2] Humphreys would later translate the socioreligious ideas inherited from his father and learned at Yale into a conservative political credo.

Despite his social, religious, and educational orthodoxy, Humphreys was also surprisingly responsive to innovation. He was influenced, for example, by new directions in the study of oratory. Throughout the last half of the eighteenth century, syllogistic disputation with its standardized Latin forms was yielding at Yale and elsewhere to forensic disputation, performed in English without the formal restraints and standardizations that had formerly prevailed.[3] Part of the revolutionary aspect of this change lay in the allowance of "ethical and pathetic" modes in logical debate, which made forensic disputation into an oral and rhetorical exercise demanding new skills in addition to logic. English grammar and composition as well as practice in speech-making became essential studies. The mounting student interest in oratory resulted in 1767, Humphreys' first year at Yale, in an extracurricular study of the subject under the general advisership of Mix Mitchell, one of the new tutors that year. The text used was John Ward's *System of Oratory* (1759).

The assault on classicism in the field of disputation was paralleled in the area of poetry and belles lettres by John Trumbull and Timothy Dwight, and very soon afterward, by David Humphreys.[4] All three were instrumental in the development of new courses in English literature at Yale, thus helping to legitimate a study that had formerly been held in contempt. David Humphreys, therefore, supported innovations in two important areas of the Yale curriculum.

Humphreys' experience in applying for membership into Yale's established literary society, the Honorable Fellowship, demonstrates further his independent turn of mind. In 1767, after being rejected by the Fellowship because he was a freshman, Humphreys organized several others from each class and formed a competing society, the

Brothers in Unity. The Brothers soon developed into a literary and dramatic as well as a debating organization, and David Humphreys emerged as a key member of the group, being put forward in all orations and debating contests as the representative of his class.[5]

The image of David Humphreys through his Yale years is that of a rather conservative young gentleman, aristocratic in bearing, who had absorbed his father's religious orthodoxy and attended fairly traditional classes at college. At the same time, however, he was in the vanguard of curriculum reform and was instrumental in the formation of an upstart new literary society. Finally, he was moved by the spirit of the time, a spirit which, in a few short years, would transform this "aristocrat" into a "revolutionary" in Washington's army.

From a literary standpoint the most important aspect of Humphreys' Yale years was his study of John Ward's *System of Oratory.* Either through extracurricular study with Mix Mitchell or through his activities in the Brothers in Unity—or through both—David Humphreys studied what Ward termed "general elocution": elegance, composition, and dignity.[6] The oratorical formulas provided by Ward served Humphreys throughout his literary career; in fact, theoretical and practical training in oratory prepared him to write a highly stylized verse built almost exclusively on the principles of "general elocution." Ward had followed the lead of ancient rhetoricians in emphasizing *inventio* and *dispositio,* the selecting and organizing of material, and, despite increasing attention paid at Yale in the last half of the eighteenth century to *elocutio* and *pronuntiato,* style and delivery, Humphreys never permitted them to dominate his subject matter. On the other hand, he also learned from Ward to reach for the sublime by using heightened rhetoric, necessitated as he thought by noble and dignified themes. In all, then, Humphreys' forensics training taught him to emphasize reason and order, but as a poet he sought to bring vividness of expression and craftsmanship into the formula.

David Humphreys achieved a wide contemporary success mixing oratory and poetry. It was, in fact, common for poetry written in America between 1750 and 1800 to be based on principles of classical rhetoric, alternately called oratory or elocution. Philosophically it valued common sense and rationalism higher than imagination and fancy. Poetry and elocution alike were persuasive arts used in the pursuit of virtue, and, in the case of David Humphreys, patriotism was the virtuous pursuit.[7] He put it this way in the "Advertisement" to "A Poem on the Love of Country" (4 July 1799): "To make use of poetry for strengthening patriotism, promoting virtue, and extending happiness, is to bring it back to its primitive employments."[8]

Humphreys wrote what is known as epideictic poetry, a highly stylized form adapted from classical rhetoric and elocution. Epideictic oratory, according to Gordon Bigelow, "implies definite occasion and audience and a dominant purpose of praise or blame, along with a highly ornamental style." In classical rhetoric "epideictic speeches, because they had no developed argument, dropped away the divisions of proposition, proof, or disproof, and were commonly divided into exordium, an extended narration which comprised the main body of the speech, and a peroration."[9] Stylistically, Humphreys was ornamental; that is, he most often tried for the sublime because, as he had learned from Ward, dignified subjects demanded sublime language. To achieve this, Humphreys relied on standard formulas, including the use of earthquakes, stormy seas, thunder and lightning, roaring winds, cannon volleys, etc. Anything grand and mighty was sufficient. Moreover, the proper method to attain heightened effects was through circumlocution, inversion, epithet, poetic diction, and strong figures: personification, apostrophe, exclamation, and interrogation.[10] The epideictic tradition, then, is the oratorical and poetic format that David Humphreys learned at Yale and later adopted as his own.

After leaving Yale in 1771, Humphreys took a position for two years as master of the school in Wethersfield, Connecticut, taking the place of John Trumbull, who had recently been appointed tutor at Yale.[11] Very few records of Humphreys' time at Wethersfield still exist, but it is known that he taught arithmetic, English literature, rhetoric and logic, and, for the college bound, elementary Latin and Greek.

Humphreys' experience teaching in the public school no doubt prepared him well for his next tutorship—at Philipse Manor. Specifically, Humphreys was tutor to the younger of Colonel Frederick

Philipse's eleven children. Here again, few details of Humphreys' three-year tenure have survived.[12] Despite the scarcity of records, however, one may note two likely results of his association with the Philipse family. First, he absorbed the polished manners of one of New York's wealthiest and most respectable families. Indeed, the affable young tutor may frequently have been accepted as a member of the family. In some measure Humphreys' aristocratic bearing— later reinforced by his long association with the Washington family and, still later, with the courts at Lisbon and Madrid—was given an early stimulus at Philipse Manor. Second, if the young man's head was turned by the nearness of Philipse society, it was not similarly turned by Philipse politics. That is, Humphreys maintained his independent turn of mind by not following his employer into the Loyalist camp. One may reasonably conclude that two of David Humphreys' most prominent characteristics, his social grace and his habit of independent thinking, were encouraged by his experience at Philipse Manor.

"Genuine Effusions"

Humphreys continued his studies independently at Wethersfield and was awarded the Master of Arts degree from Yale in 1774. His oration on "Taste" has not survived; nonetheless, his excellent academic reputation, his friendship with Trumbull and Dwight, and his teaching experience led to his invitation by Yale in 1775 to be a tutor. This he declined. Probably he had already decided against an academic career, despite the fact that he was then, and continued to be for some time afterward, a tutor. Regardless of his actual vocation, however, his affection for Yale and his friends there as well as his commitment to literature and language insured that he would continue with his poetic avocation. As it happened, the Revolution became a fighting war, and Humphreys' future began to take shape when he volunteered for military service; the Revolution provided the perfect growth medium for Humphreys as patriot and poet. His military service was the first of several careers throughout his life which revealed his eighteenth-century gentleman's obligation, in a grand and aristocratic style, to serve the commonweal. Throughout them all he was a poet.

Just before he joined the army in New York during the late summer of 1776, Humphreys wrote his earliest known poems, Sonnet I ("Addressed to my Friends at Yale College, on my leaving them to join the Army") and "An Ode, to his Excellency Gen'r¹ Washington." These early poems tell a great deal about Humphreys as a poet.

Sonnet I appears to have been written by early or mid-1776, although there is no record of its publication until the 1804 *Miscellaneous Works*.

> Adieu, thou Yale! where youthful poets dwell,
> No more I linger by thy classic stream.
> Inglorious ease and sportive songs farewell!
> Thou startling clarion! break the sleeper's dream!
>
> And sing, ye bards! the war-inspiring theme.
> Heard ye the din of battle? clang of arms?
> Saw ye the steel 'mid starry banners beam?
> Quick throbs my breast at war's untried alarms,
> Unknown pulsations stirr'd by glory's charms.
>
> While dear Columbia calls, no danger awes,
> Though certain death to threaten'd chains be join'd.
> Though fails this flesh devote to freedom's cause,
> Can death subdue th'unconquerable mind?
> Or adamantine chains ethereal substance bind?[13]

In this sonnet, generally thought to be among America's first, Humphreys bids "adieu" to Yale and the "youthful poets" who had been his friends. In reality, of course, he had not been living at Yale since his graduation in 1771, but Humphreys could not overlook the literary possibilities which the dramatic posture of poet-turned-warrior afforded him. He turned from "inglorious ease" and "sportive songs" to matters of far greater importance: "the war-inspiring theme." In an unusually self-revealing couplet he wrote: "Quick throbs my breast at war's untried alarms, / Unknown pulsations stirr'd by glory's charms." He concluded that the spirit of freedom cannot be killed or bound by chains: "While dear Columbia calls, no danger awes."

David Humphreys' first known poem reveals the two most salient characteristics of his personality, namely, passions for poetry and patriotism. Significantly, the poem announces not that he will give up poetry, but that he will give up his bucolic existence for a military one. Humphreys did not feel forced to turn away from the muse because of the Revolution. With what talents he possessed Humphreys wrote verses occasioned by the war, hoping that they might uplift and inspire. A one-to-one relationship existed between poetry and patriotism.

In form and content Sonnet I is simple and direct. Its principal structural design is supplied by the epideictic speech, adapted to a poetic format. Instead of employing either the Shakespearean or Italian sonnet forms, Humphreys chose a unique three-part structure, one quatrain followed by two quintains. This three-part structure corresponds loosely to the format of the epideictic speech with its exordium, narration, and peroration. The opening quatrain, the exordium, is designed to catch the reader's attention and introduce the subject. Here Humphreys announced that the "startling clarion" has broken his "sleeper's dream" and that he must therefore leave the "classic stream." In stanza two, the narration, Humphreys announced the facts, simply that the "clang of arms" and the "starry banners" stir "unknown pulsations" within him. He has given up "inglorious ease" for "glory's charms." The final stanza, the peroration, is an emotional reaffirmation of the patriotic rightness of his decision. Not even "certain death" could deter him "while dear Columbia calls." "Freedom's cause" will not die. The patriotic theme is bolstered throughout by the preponderance of apostrophe, exclamation, and interrogation, the strong figures frequently used in patriotic oratory. Moreover, Humphreys pursued the grand style, the sublime, relying—rather unimaginatively—on stock images: "startling clarion," "din of battle," and "clang of arms."

This early poem shows that David Humphreys was first a patriot, a man with a public conscience. Equally clear is that poetry was his chosen avocation, and, because he viewed his poetry as a means of promoting public virtue, the two became inseparable. Humphreys did forsake the academy for a military career, but he also commemorated the decision in verse—an encomium to the spirit of freedom.

A third thing is also clear: Sonnet I is a technical product of oratory in design and characteristic, a miniature epideictic speech set in sonnet form. Although some of the details change, an ardent nationalism which expresses itself in public service and an oratorical poetry identify David Humphreys throughout his several careers.

Another example of this pattern at work, again in a fairly short, early poem is "An Ode to his Excellency Gen'r¹ Washington." This poem reveals the same themes and techniques observable in Sonnet I, but it is also Humphreys' first panegyric poem.[14]

> To Washington, who greatly brave,
> Resolv'd his native land to save,
>   Or perish in the cause:
> To Washington, what praise belongs!
> What marble busts! what grateful songs!
>   What tributes of applause!
>
> At freedom's call, the Hero rose,
> Left each dear scene, & sought our foes,
>   And brav'd their fiercest rage:
> While they (for us a scourge design'd)
> Within their walls inglorious pin'd,
>   Nor dar'd with him engage.
>
> His martial skill our legions form'd,
> His glorious zeal their bosoms warm'd,
>   And fann'd the rising flame,
> Like Fabius, he by wise delay,
> Forc'd Britains bands to waste away,
>   Then bade them fly with shame.
>
> His Vengeance struck them with dismay,
> His thunders broke their firm array,
>   And wither'd all the host.
> Why felt thy chiefs unusual dread?
> Where were thy sons O Britain fled,
>   To what ill-fated coast?
>
> But now the cannon's thundering roar,
> Begins to echo round the shore,

And calls our youths from far.
Oh! now may he, with glory crown'd,
While guardian Angels shield him round,
Tryumphant guide the war.

At last (for so the fates decreed)
These climes by him from slav'ry freed,
And ev'ry wrong redrest—
While grateful Myriads hail his name,
May he bright heir of deathless fame,
Long live supremely blest.

Humphreys sent a copy of the poem to Col. Samuel B. Webb, then an aide of Washington, hoping the General would see it. In the letter accompanying the poem, dated 8 July 1776, Humphreys assumed the authorial posture that he maintained throughout the remainder of his life: "The subject is a noble one, & he must be a stupid fellow, who couldn't say one clever thing upon it—how I have succeeded you must determine,—this may be said in its favour, or rather by way of excuse for its imperfections, that it contains the genuine effusions of an honest & grateful heart, & that it was the employment of only half an hour."[15] As this letter suggests, Humphreys considered the subject of a poem to be more important than the poem itself. Moreover, it was also characteristic of David Humphreys—and his age—to show a becoming modesty, deferring always to others for judgment. At the same time, however, the letter has a tone of self-assurance, a feeling that his work was bound to be received well, and, for the most part—during his lifetime, at least—it was. Also typical of Humphreys is that he should excuse the imperfections of his work because "it was the employment of only half an hour." Humphreys wished always to present himself as a gentleman whose poetic efforts were nothing more than the happy products of his spare moments. His more important work, of course, was serving the public. His were the "genuine effusions of an honest heart," and, insofar as his "effusions" served the public good, he considered himself successful as a poet.

The ode to Washington shows a young man's patriotic enthusiasm. Its form is epideictic. The first stanza is the exordium, which introduces the subject: brave Washington, who "Resolv'd his native land to save," deserves commemoration in art, specifically in busts and songs—"tributes of applause." Clearly Humphreys meant his own poem to help fill the void. The middle three stanzas constitute the narration. They show Washington volunteering to serve his country, demonstrating "martial skill" and "glorious zeal." The final two stanzas, the peroration, add a slight emotional appeal to the loose "argument." Washington deserves commemoration not only for his "skill" and "zeal," but also for having saved "these climes" from slavery. In the peroration, too, Humphreys reached out for the sublime by calling up "the cannon's thundering roar." Furthermore, he employed the strong figures of apostrophe, exclamation, and interrogation—all borrowed from patriotic oratory. As he had learned from Ward, panegyric poems "naturally admit of all the ornaments and assistance of eloquence."[16]

Since the ode was not published at the time it was written (and appears never to have been printed during Humphreys' lifetime), it had no effect whatever on the public good. Perhaps for this reason Humphreys did not value the poem very highly, for he seems quite deliberately to have omitted it from any later collection. Perhaps, too, he simply lost track of it. Regardless, this poem confirms the pattern of Humphreys' writing in his later, more important works: he chose a patriotic subject; he viewed the poem as being less important than its subject; and he approached the verse in form and content as a variation of the oratorical formulas he had studied at Yale.

Chapter Two
Soldier

David Humphreys enjoyed a distinguished military career, rising rapidly from captain in 1777 to lieutenant colonel in 1780. More significant even than his rise in rank was his service under three generals as aide-de-camp, a position important both in field and cabinet service. Contemporary and subsequent historical accounts agree that Humphreys was naturally suited to the military; his skill, dedication, and genuine patriotism recommended him as an officer with superior abilities. During the war years Humphreys also managed to complete a number of patriotic poems. The most important of these is the "Address to the Armies" (1778–82), but he also wrote "Elegy on the Burning of Fairfield" (1780), "Elegy on Lieutenant de Hart" (1780), and Sonnets II, III, and IV. In addition, Humphreys wrote a fine light poem, "Letter to a Young Lady in Boston" (1780), and an almost totally unknown poem, "The Farewell" (1782). Each of these poems was occasioned by the war and reveals perfectly Humphreys' dual passions—patriotism and poetry.

The War

It was August 1776 when Humphreys joined the army in New York. He was then a volunteer adjutant with the rank of captain in the second Connecticut regiment, a position which gave him good experience and paved the way for similar appointments later. Although Humphreys was not present at the disastrous battle of Long Island, he was among the five thousand troops Washington left near the East River to occupy the British while the regiments and military stores were being removed to Harlem Heights. This troop movement on 15 September 1776 cost the Americans thirty killed and one hundred wounded; it was the first military action that David Humphreys saw.[1] Many years later, he described the scene: "Before our brigade came in, we were given up for lost by all our friends. So critical indeed was our situation, and so narrow the gap by which we escaped, that the instant we had passed the enemy closed it by extending their line from river to river."[2]

After the retreat, Humphreys experienced the first of many frustrating interruptions of his military service. Washington, describing the second Connecticut militia as being reduced to "almost nothing," discharged the entire regiment on 24 September, thus returning Humphreys to his home. He once again volunteered, however, this time for a three-year service with the sixth Connecticut regiment; in March 1777, though, he was named brigade-major of General Samuel Parsons' first brigade of the Connecticut Line. His primary responsibility with Parsons was the mustering and equipping of new troops scheduled to go to the Hudson in early summer.

Humphreys' second experience in military combat came on 21 May 1777. On that date Colonel Return Meigs led a force of 234 men, including Major David Humphreys, on a raid of British stores at Sag Harbor. Meigs's force destroyed twelve supply schooners; six British soldiers were killed and ninety were taken prisoner. There were no American casualties. David Humphreys was chosen by General Parsons as the messenger to report the success of the raid to George Washington. In a letter to Washington, dated 25 May 1777, Parsons said: "Major Humphreys, who waits on your Excellency with the account, was in the action with Col. Meigs, and will be able to give any further necessary information."[3] This is the first known meeting between George Washington and David Humphreys, although Washington may have remembered Humphreys as the author of an ode, probably shown to him nine months earlier.

By 2 July Parsons and his men were reassigned to Peekskill, where they spent the summer waiting, drilling, and strengthening defenses. The overall operations in the Hudson Highlands were under the direction of Israel Putnam, who had assumed command in May. Humphreys later assayed the military situation that summer as a period of uncertainty and tension: "The gathering tempests menaced the northern frontiers, the posts in the Highlands, and the city of Philadelphia; but it was still doubtful where the fury of the storm would fall."[4] After the September to October loss of Forts Montgomery and Clinton, Washington instructed Putnam in a letter of 2 December "to employ your whole force and all the means in your power for erecting and completing such works and obstructions as may be necessary to defend the river."[5] The site selected was West Point. On 20 January General Parsons' brigade began construction of the permanent works.

With the memory still strong of the successful outcome of Meigs's raid in May of the preceding year, Humphreys undertook the command of a similar, though smaller, expedition in the latter part of February 1778. He led a group of thirty volunteers down to a Long Island shore point near Smithtown. There he intended to destroy a large British man-of-war which had run aground; unfortunately the ship had been set afloat and left the area shortly before Humphreys and his men arrived. The party did destroy three British vessels—a brig, a schooner, and a sloop—before returning to West Point with no casualties.

During the spring and early summer of 1778, Humphreys remained with General Parsons' brigade in the Highlands. In August he was part of an unsuccessful attempt to take Newport with a combination of New England troops and the French fleet. After the failure in Rhode Island, the American forces went into winter quarters. Shortly afterward, on 17 December 1778, Humphreys was honored again, this time by being appointed aide-de-camp to General Putnam. He joined the general's military family at its headquarters near Danbury, Connecticut.

Putnam was at that time in command of the forces around Redding. Late in February 1779, Putnam, while on an inspection of the outpost at Horse Neck, was surprised by a force of 1,500 men under Governor William Tryon. Humphreys later related the story of Putnam's escape in the following romanticized fashion:

About the middle of winter, while General Putnam was on a visit to his out-post at Horse-Neck, he found Governor Tryon advancing upon that town with a corps of fifteen hundred men. To oppose these General Putnam had only a picquet of one hundred and fifty men, and two iron field-pieces, without horses or dragropes. . . . He ordered the picquet to provide for their safety, by retiring to a swamp inaccessible to horse, and secured his own, by plunging down the steep precipice at the church upon a full trot. This precipice is so steep, where he descended, as to have artificial stairs, composed of nearly one hundred stone steps, for the accommodation of foot passengers. There the Dragoons, who were but a sword's length from him, stopped short; for the declivity was so abrupt, that they ventured not to follow; and, before they could gain the valley, by going round the brow of the hill in the ordinary road, he was far enough beyond their reach.[6]

Even if this episode was rather less exciting or heroic than Humphreys made it out to be, it was still exceptional; for Putnam and his military family were, for the most part, involved in routine and uneventful work.

Putnam commanded the Maryland line at Buttermilk Falls, two miles below West Point, during the campaign of 1779. His official charge was to continue strengthening the works at West Point, to prevent Clinton from obtaining control of important points on the river. Humphreys had joined Putnam in the twilight of the old general's career, at a time when Washington no longer gave him key strategic commands; and thus the campaign of 1779 passed for David Humphreys at a considerable distance from the action.

Hiatus

Sir Henry Clinton and the hated Governor Tryon plundered New Haven on 6 July 1779, taking forty-five prisoners. Part of Clinton's Connecticut Coast Raid included the burning of Fairfield, approximately twenty miles from New Haven. Nearly two hundred homes, barns, and storehouses, plus two schools, two churches, the jail, and the courthouse, were all burned to the ground. Among the homes destroyed was that of Sarah Humphreys Mills, Humphreys' only sister. When Humphreys visited the site late in the fall of 1779, the ruins impressed him both from a personal and military standpoint and motivated him to write "Elegy on the Burning of Fairfield."

Meanwhile, Putnam was scheduled in late 1779 to join Washington at his winter headquarters in Morristown. In December, however, while en route to Morristown, Putnam suffered a paralytic stroke that kept him and his aides in Connecticut and ultimately forced the retirement of the old general. Putnam's stroke gave David Humphreys an unexpected and extended leave, which he spent primarily in New Haven. This hiatus resulted in a flurry of literary activity. Not only did he write "Elegy on the Burning of Fairfield," but he also revised the "Poem Addressed to the Armies of the United States." During the early months of 1780 he wrote Sonnet II ("On the Revolutionary War in America") and "Letter to a Young Lady in Boston." Regarding this literary productivity, Humphreys wrote somewhat playfully to Nathaniel Greene: "Now what could induce me to turn Scribbler, whether my own Sins, or those of my Parents (as Pope says) must be left to further discussion; tho I rather imagine the mischief, like a thousand others, will be found, to have originated, in a great measure, from keeping ill Company; such as . . . Col⁰ Wadsworth, a certain Mʳ Trumbull, a Mʳ Dwight, a Doctʳ Styles, & some other similar Characters, of smaller notoriety— These men are enough to corrupt half the youth of the States and introduce them to the same evil practices."[7]

Humphreys said in *Miscellaneous Works (1804)* that the "Elegy on the Burning of Fairfield" was "Written in 1779, on the Spot where the Town stood." This, however, is unlikely. In a letter to Nathaniel Greene in April 1780, Humphreys wrote that the poem "was written to indulge, a pleasing kind of melancholly, and while away a vacant hour the other morning."[8] And, in a letter to Jeremiah Wadsworth, dated New Haven 30 March 1780, he wrote, "the Elegy on the burning of Fairfield, was the work of a few liesure minutes, the other day."[9] Humphreys may have spoken very loosely when he said that the poem was written "the other morning" and "the other day," so loosely, in fact, as to allow for a late 1779 composition. It is more likely, however, that he confused the moment of inspiration with the moment of composition; no doubt the idea for the poem came to him when he visited Fairfield in the autumn of 1779, but it is unlikely he wrote it before March 1780.

The "Elegy on the Burning of Fairfield" evokes both pity and anger and is, overall, fairly successful, even though its sixteen-quatrain stanzas of iambic pentameter rely too heavily on apostrophe, exaggeration, and exclamation. The poem has a one-stanza exordium, a one-stanza peroration, and a fourteen-stanza narration. Stanzas two through five contain a melancholy look at the ruins of the town, made gloomier by the recollection of what it had been shortly before. But in stanzas six through fifteen the subject of the poem is Governor Tryon. Humphreys called up horrible images of the town's destruction and the people's suffering in order to show his readers precisely what Tryon was responsible for. The theme of the "Elegy" is to lament the loss of the town to the ravages of war, but in so doing, Humphreys was also able to add a political dimension by enraging readers to Tryon's cruelties. The poet's righteous outrage culminates in two rhetorical questions, well placed for oratorical effect:

> Could Tryon hope to quench the patriot flame
>> Or make his deeds survive in glory's page?
> Could Britons seek of savages the fame,
>> Or deem it conquest, thus the war to wage? (*MW*, 29–32)

The Britons have indeed "insulted" the Americans, the poet says, to "tenfold vengeance." The poem ends with an emotional flourish, a suitable climax for a poem that has been building in outrage from the opening line:

> These be thy triumphs! this thy boasted fame!
>> Daughters of mem'ry, raise the deathless songs!
> Repeat through endless years his hated name,
>> Embalm his crimes, and teach the world our wrongs. (*MW*, 61–64)

The "Elegy" was widely reprinted for the next twenty years, and Humphreys justifiably assumed a small part of the credit for the widespread association of Tryon's name with savage cruelty.

Similar in tone and content to the Fairfield "Elegy" is Humphreys' Sonnet II, "On the Revolutionary War in America." The composition of this poem is impossible to date exactly, but its kinship to the Fairfield "Elegy" makes an early 1780 composition likely.[10] This sonnet, like the first, is written in a three-part, epideictic movement, with an opening quatrain and two following quintains in iambic pentameter. The only formal difference between the first and the second sonnets is in the rhyme scheme. In Sonnet I Humphreys introduced two new rhymes in the final quintain, while in Sonnet II he recalled at the end two rhymes from stanza one. The new arrangement produced a superior closure and argues that Humphreys was striving to achieve a tighter structural unity. The "Elegy" with its anger and bitter denunciations of Tryon had been a public poem and was probably followed by the more private sonnet, which, by its resignation to the "exterminating angel," reveals a greater sense of brooding and uncertainty. The private sonnet may be said to reveal more intimately than the public "Elegy" Humphreys' deepest fears and anxieties. In his public utterances Humphreys wanted to be encouraging and inspirational, while in private he showed a greater sobriety—even discouragement.

A contrast to the gravity of tone and content in the "Elegy" and Sonnet II is Humphreys' "Letter to a Young Lady in Boston," an amusing poem written for the most part with ease, grace, and good humor. Humphreys appears to have given himself up to this poem only after his more serious work had been tended to, for not only had he by then finished the "Address to the Armies," the "Elegy," and Sonnet II, but he had also eliminated the uncertainty of his military future by securing an invitation to join the staff of the Commander-in-Chief. It is no wonder that he felt in good humor as he wrote the "Letter."

The "Letter" is written in twenty-two irregular stanzas—217 lines in all—of iambic verse with feminine endings. Both the meter and the double and triple rhymes contribute to the lightness and humor of the poem. The overall effect, while imperfect in execution, is genuinely amusing; the poet displays both wit and craftsmanship as he moves skillfully around the edges of the mock-heroic form. But the poem also has its serious moments, particularly the last six stanzas (68 lines). Stanza seventeen is devoted to General Putnam, whose illness had given Humphreys his first full-time opportunity to write. Stanza twenty contains brief notice of his New Haven friends: Trumbull, Barlow, and Dwight. At the end of the "Letter," the war brought Humphreys back to the darker realities of the real world. New Haven, after all, contained only memories of youth. Those must now be "For ever lost, in civil strife." The war also brought the poet back to the sublime style, for he heard "The cannon's distant thunders" and bade "Adieu" to New Haven and "the scenes that charm'd my view." The poem ends with a typical flourish:

> My country's cause in my soul invades—
> Yes, rous'd by sense of country's wrongs,
> I give the wind my idle songs:
> No vacant hour for rhyme succeeds,
> I go where'er the battle bleeds:
> To-morrow—(brief then be my story)—
> I go to WASHINGTON and GLORY;
> His Aide-de-Camp—in acts when tried—
> Resolv'd (whatever fates betide)
> My conduct, till my final breath,
> Shall not disgrace my life or death. (*MW*, 207–17)

Despite the inflated self-awareness of these lines (the excitement over his appointment was too strong to be subdued), the poem's amusing narrative and catalogue of Connecticut notables earn for it an overall appeal that is difficult to deny.

The "Elegy," Sonnet II, and the "Letter" are all interesting performances, but the most ambitious and important poem that Humphreys wrote during the winter of 1779–80—certainly the one that gave the greatest impetus to his several careers—was the "Address to the Armies." This poem gained such a wide currency in America and France that it was translated in 1785–86 into French by one of the philosophes, the Marquis de Chastellux. Since the "Address" is the first of Humphreys' long works and because it is representative in both style and content, it requires special attention.

From Hartford on 23 May, Humphreys had sent advance copies of the "Address" to George Washington and Nathaniel Greene. In the cover letter to Greene he characteristically remarked, "So far as an honest intention, and a zeal for my Country can be urg'd in excuse for indifferent Poetry, I am determin'd to claim the indulgence of the Public in general, and the patronage of my friends in particular."[11] The poem itself is a verse oration written in 466 lines of regular heroic couplets, a suitable form for a poem intended, from one standpoint at least, as a glowing tribute to the "heroic" American forces. [12] It begins with two verse epigraphs. The first is from Horace:

> Soon faithfulness, and peace, and honor
> And revered modesty; and neglected virtue
> Will dare to return; and soon a blessed
> Horn of plenty will appear. [13]

Horace speaks of the paradisiac age of Saturn returning, bringing with it peace and honor. The second is a single line from Virgil, "The great months will begin to proceed," a reference to the messianic child who is to usher in a new and perfect era. Humphreys borrowed the lines to link the post-Revolutionary War "paradise" in America with that predicted by the Latin poets, an auspicious beginning for both country and poem.

The poem is addressed in the first line, with Humphreys' typically heightened rhetoric, to "martial bands! Columbia's fairest pride!" These soldiers, "gallant youths! whose breasts for glory burn," are urged to "attend" the "hallow'd theme": "The past review; the future scene explore, / And Heav'n's high King with grateful hearts adore!" (*MW*, 11–12). The first twelve lines constitute the exordium of the poem: Humphreys appealed to the patriotism of the soldiers "who, unmov'd, in the dread hour stood." In the name of their noblest and most patriotic sentiments, Humphreys invited the "martial bands" to view both their past and future. Individuals are urged to spurn "Each selfish aim and meaner passion."

The exordium provides more than a simple introduction; rather, it is an impassioned appeal to the "gallant youths," "Who greatly dar'd, at Freedom's rapt'rous call, / With her to triumph, or with her to fall—" (*MW*, 7–8). Moreover, by surveying past events and peering into the future, the exordium also recalls the standard book of the underworld where, for example, Odysseus and Aeneas were granted similar experiences. Humphreys was appealing, through this parallel, to a "heroic" or epic spirit in America; that is, his scenes of the Revolution hold a special, mythological, significance to the beginnings of the new American nation. The exordium in the "Address," then, shows a complex richness of design, texture, and purpose, a richness suggestive of what is to follow in the extended narration.

The narration consists of many verse paragraphs surveying the past and future; however, the greater part is devoted to a patriotic review of the Revolution (330 lines) followed by a briefer prophetic vision (97 lines). Humphreys' review of the war included an opening diatribe against the British, a tribute to the American soldiers who volunteered, a sketch of the first battle, the arrival of George Washington, the laments for three heroes who died, the call for American writers to memorialize British cruelties and American victories, the constant need for a vigilant perseverance, the rejoicing that accompanied independence, and the happiness occasioned by news of the peace.

In the opening diatribe against England Humphreys defended America. England, he said, had "Frown'd on her sons, and bade them turn to slaves—": "The parent state—a parent now no more— / Let loose the hirelings of despotic power" (MW, 17–18). This emotional appeal serves loosely to identify the enemy, but more importantly, it legitimates the American call to arms. When England turned its "sons" to "slaves," America, Humphreys implied, had every right to resort to force, resisting "the hirelings of despotic power."

Humphreys presented a tribute to American volunteers at Concord, where "fell our brothers, by fierce ruffians slain." The result of that action, according to Humphreys, and the exaggeration suited his purpose because it was consistent with his sense of the sublime, was a spontaneous, colony-wide war effort:

> Then the shrill trumpet echo'd from afar,
> And sudden blaz'd the wasting flame of war;
> From State to State, swift flew the dire alarms,
> And ardent youths, impetuous, rush'd to arms:
> "To arms" the matrons and the virgins sung,
> To arms, their sires, their husbands, brothers sprung.
> No dull delay—where'er the sound was heard,
> Where the red standards in the air appear'd,
> Where, through vast realms, the cannon swell'd its roar,
> Between th' Acadian and Floridian shore. (MW, 29–38)

Between the first published version of this poem in 1780 and the second in 1782, Humphreys betrayed a somewhat more sober understanding of the difficulties of raising an army: "The Recruits come in very slowly from the Eastern States.—A strange lethargy seems to have seized all Ranks & orders of men—Unless great exertions are made, our Reg^{ts} will be very weak this campaign."[14] Humphreys' exaggeration about the American willingness to serve in the Continental Army, an exaggeration that verges on myth-making, was in part the result of what he saw as his purpose in the poem: "To inspire our countrymen, now in arms, or who may hereafter be called into the field, with perseverance and fortitude, through every species of difficulty and danger, to continue their exertions for the defence of their country, and the preservation of its liberties, is the object of this address."[15] This reveals quite clearly Humphreys' aim, here and elsewhere, which was to write a public kind of inspirational poetry.

The poem depicts the action at Charlestown and Bunker Hill, culminating with the death of Joseph Warren.

> Long rag'd the contest on th'embattled field;
> Nor those would fly, nor these would tamely yield—
> Till Warren fell, in all the boast of arms,
> The pride of genius and unrivall'd charms,
> His country's hope!—full soon the gloom was spread:
> Oppress'd with numbers, and their leader dead,
> Slow from the field the sullen troops retir'd;
> Behind, the hostile flame to heav'n aspir'd. (*MW*, 53–60)

The death of Warren represents the dramatic nadir of the war—at least for the sake of the poem: "Now darkness gather'd round; / The thunder rumbled, and the tempest frown'd." The poem's dramatic turning point occurs when George Washington enters: "When lo! to guide us through the storm of war, / Beam'd the bright splendour of Virginia's star" (*MW*, 67–68). Washington's "voice inspir'd, his godlike presence led. / The Britons saw, and from his presence fled" (*MW*, 85–86). Such deification of Washington suited Humphreys' literary plan; that is, exaggeration is consistent with the epic parallels which frame the poem. Humphreys sought to memorialize the history of the American nation by identifying that history with a single heroic—even godlike—figure: George Washington was transformed into the mythological founder of a new nation.

Washington parallels epic heroes in that he entered the war as a combatant precisely at the moment of greatest gloom, just as Achilles entered the Trojan War when all seemed hopeless for the Greeks. (If it is agreed that the loss at Bunker Hill was not the nadir of the American war effort, then it is also to be admitted that the historical facts have been bent for literary purposes, a practice which bothered Humphreys no more than Virgil.) Moreoever, Humphreys believed the Commander-in-Chief needed to be raised to heroic proportions, particularly to the soldiers in the field. Such an image, he believed, would promote the most unified national spirit possible.

Following the dramatic introduction of George Washington into the poem, Humphreys proceeded to memorialize three American heroes who had died in the war: John Brown, Alexander Scammel, and John Laurens. These three symbolize all the American casualties. The emotional recollection of their deaths, accompanied always by long apostrophes and numerous exclamations, reached a level of the sublime that Humphreys found extremely moving. Brown is called "hapless friend!" because he and Humphreys were indeed old college friends, both graduating in the class of 1771 at Yale. Humphreys praised Brown's "force of limbs, the mind so well inform'd, / The taste refin'd, the breast with friendship warm'd" (MW, 101–102). Humphreys was appalled at the horror of Brown's death: "the dark bands from thee, expiring, tore / Thy long hair mingled with the spouting gore" (MW, 105–106). Scammel, forced to surrender his patrol to the British at Yorktown, had been summarily murdered by his captors: "Fell chance betray'd thee to the hostile band, / The hapless victim of th'assassin hand!"[16] (MW, 111–12). The last hero in Humphreys' pantheon is John Laurens. In a combination of exclamations and questions, both in the form of apostrophe, Humphreys recalled the fact that Laurens had been wounded twice earlier in the war—at Germantown in October 1777 and at Monmouth in June 1778:

> O Laurens! gen'rous youth! twice hadst thou bled;
> Could not the ball with devious aim have sped?
> And must thy friends, now peace appears so near,
> Weep the third stroke that cuts a life so dear;
> That blots the prospect of our rising morn,
> And leaves thy country, as thy sire, forlorn? (*MW*, 129–34)

Humphreys called all three "Companions lov'd!" and concluded his lament with, "Oft will I drop the tributary tear."

The patriotism of Brown, Scammel, and Laurens links heroism and art:

> For soon their deeds, illustrious, shall be shown
> In breathing bronze, or animated stone,
> Or where the canvass, starting into life,
> Revives the glories of the crimson strife. (*MW*, 149–52)

More important than sculpture or painting for Humphreys is, of course, poetry, and the next hundred lines are framed by his call for a poet to commemorate not just the heroes, but the British and Hessian cruelties as well as the American victories:

> Columbia calls—her parent voice demands
> More grateful off'rings from your filial hands.
> And soon some bard shall tempt the untry'd themes,
> Sing how we dar'd, in Fortune's worst extremes[.] (*MW*, 157–60)

The bard should sing of "cruel wrongs," "various ills," and "boding terrors." He should sing of "British legions, arm'd with death-like pow'r" and "fierce Germania," whose battalions "Spread death around: where'er your eyes ye turn'd, / Fled were the peasants, and the village burn'd" (*MW*, 169–70). The bard should help Americans to remember always "others' suff'rings," the "tort'ring pangs your bleeding country felt!" Remember, too, he reminded the soldiers, that the British are trying to "quench your name, as though it ne'er had been." Humphreys mentioned these details as the subject of poetic efforts in the future, but they are also the actual subject of his own poem. The emotional nationalism of the "Address" was designed to promote unity and spirit among the frequently disheartened Continental forces.

Beyond the British and German cruelties, the bard will also write about the various American victories, like Washington's at Trenton:

> Where the great chief, o'er Del'ware's icey wave,
> Led the small band, in danger doubly brave;
> On high designs, and ere the dawning hour,
> Germania's vet'rans own'd the victor's pow'r[.][17] (*MW*, 213–16)

Heroes like Hugh Mercer, Horatio Gates, and Anthony Wayne are remembered for the battles at Princeton, Saratoga, and Stoney Point. Four lines commemorate Nathaniel Greene:

> Now turn your eyes, where southern realms are seen,
> From ruin rescu'd, by th'immortal Greene:
> See toils of death, where many a hero bleeds,
> Till rapid vict'ry, to defeat, succeeds. (*MW*, 229–32)

The catalogue of American victories is capped by a seventeen-line recounting of the surrender of Cornwallis at Yorktown, "on fair Virginia's strand." Lord Cornwallis surrendered the standards on 20 October 1781 and Washington gave Humphreys the honor of delivering them to Congress at Philadelphia. Humphreys mentioned his own role in the surrender proceedings in the Yorktown summary:

> These twice twelve flags no more shall be display'd,
> Save in the dome where warlike spoils are laid:
> Since, where the fathers in high council meet,
> This hand has plac'd them prostrate at their feet. (*MW*, 251–54)

Throughout his life, Humphreys felt very keenly the honor of having been selected by Washington for this important mission.

The troops are shown the joys of independence, "the glorious meed of all our warlike toils." Humphreys said that independence will shed its "stern influence on our western world." Independence is represented as "stern" in the sense of "austere" because to keep independence, in Humphreys' view, the American forces must be prepared to make continued sacrifices. Their rewards, however, will be commensurate with their sufferings: "The fair reward to suff'ring virtue giv'n, / Pure robes of bliss, and starry thrones in heav'n"

(*MW*, 305–306). The subject of peace ends the first part of the narration. To maintain the formula use of the sublime, however, Humphreys must show what the formal peace has *ended:*

> The martial clarion shall be heard no more,
> Nor the loud cannon's desolating roar:
> No more our heroes pour the purple flood,
> No corse be seen with garments roll'd in blood;
> No shivering wretch shall roam without a shed;
> No pining orphans raise the cry for bread[.] (*MW*, 319–24)

Finally, Humphreys apostrophized peace in a grand and majestic conclusion to the first part of the narration: "Hail, heav'n-born Peace! thy grateful blessings pour / On this glad land."

The second part of the narration is much shorter than the first, amounting to only ninety-seven lines. Here Humphreys looked into the future to see America's beauties and invited the armies to settle in the western territories. The movement is consistent with the Horatian and Virgilian epigraphs in which paradise is associated with the faraway West. Humphreys spoke rapturously of the "fair Ohio," nature blossoming in her "virgin pride," of "rural coverts," "sunny hills," "noon-tide bow'rs," "fragrant groves," and "vernal glories." Heaven, he said, "shall bless the toil, / Your own the produce, as your own the soil." No natural disaster will mar this western paradise—there will be "No blast severe," "No vollied hail-stones," "no driving storm," and "No raging murrain." Rather, there will be "golden years" with "cloudless sunshine" gilding "salubrious plains." The fields will yield "nectareous juice" and "Delicious honey." Clearly Humphreys' design is to present images suggesting, in the Horatian and Virgilian senses, a return to paradise. The American soldiers will find their reward in land—in fact, the "promised land."

In the peroration, lines 441–66, Humphreys restated the edenic vision of the previous section and attempted to reinforce his earlier argument with an appropriate emotional appeal. Specifically, as in a laudatory oration, there is an effort to excite love of country: greatness lies waiting for the American armies if they will only bring their heroic efforts to a victorious conclusion. In an apostrophe to

God, Humphreys, speaking for the American armies as well as for himself, asked for a divine blessing to make America all that he has seen it to be:

> And thou Supreme! whose hand sustains this ball,
> Before whose nod the nations rise and fall,
> Propitious smile, and shed diviner charms
> On this blest land, the queen of arts and arms;
> Make the great empire rise on Wisdom's plan,
> The seat of bliss, and last retreat of man. (*MW*, 461–66)

Humphreys' "Address to the Armies" began with numerous commemorations of American heroes and visions of a pastoral paradise; it ended with a prayer for divine blessing. It began on a political note and ended on a religious one. His object, he had said, was "to inspire our countrymen," and at the end of his "Address" he made an appropriate appeal to the source of all inspiration. Thus Humphreys linked divine sanction to the patriot cause.

Washington and Glory

Humphreys did not join Washington as aide-de-camp "Tomorrow" as he had said he would in the "Letter to a Young Lady in Boston." He had, however, during April and May 1780, kept a correspondence with Nathaniel Greene about a position. Putnam was ill, and Humphreys—despite his feelings for the old general— was becoming impatient to resume some active part in the war effort. In one letter to Greene, dated New Haven, 10 April 1780, he stated his dissatisfaction with prolonged inactivity, thus suggesting his availability:

The ill-state of health, which has prevented our old friend the General (with whom I had the honor of serving) from returning to Camp; has likewise subjected me, to a state of *inactivity* and *rustication* for several months past; this, I should have little reason to regret, from the manner in which I have spent the time [i.e., writing], during the inactive season of the year: but the idea of its being protracted into the active parts of the Campaign, might be rather irksome & disagreeable. However I shall not make myself, or friends anxious about my situation; for if my Country should have no farther occasion for my services, I shall be perfectly willing to retire, if otherwise I make no doubt of being permitted to serve it, in such a manner as will be most conducive to the public good; which is the utmost of my ambition—[18]

Humphreys never better defined the "utmost limit" of his ambitions in public enterprise; he wished—without vanity or false modesty— to serve his country in the manner "most conducive to the public good."

Late in May 1780, Humphreys joined Greene's military family as aide-de-camp, although they must have mutually agreed that Humphreys' appointment would be temporary, since, as he had noted in his "Letter to a Young Lady in Boston," he was already anticipating his appointment to Washington's staff. On 23 May Humphreys wrote Greene: "We are this moment made happy, by the arrival of the News from your quarter, that a french fleet will be on the Coast in a few days; this, with many other things will induce me probably, to accept of the kind offer of coming into your family, in the manner you propose; for which & every other instance of your friendship, you will ever receive my most grateful acknowl- edgements."[19] With Greene and Washington, Humphreys was about to enter a more active and exciting period of wartime service.

On 30 May Humphreys wrote a long letter to Greene. One passage in particular demands attention because it isolates Humphreys' nat- urally aristocratic turn of mind. Never had he expressed such ideas as openly as in this letter. Even though "every prospect from abroad looks exceedingly favorable," for the war effort, he said, the situation at home looks far less encouraging: "The stupidity & negligence of the people at large to their own interest, the knavery of some, and the want of ability in others, who are concerned in the administration of public affairs, and especially the unbounded, uncontroulable spirit of dissipation, licentiousness, & avarice, which predominates thro every rank and order of men, so far as they have any opportunity for its gratification; afford the most gloomy presage of what the event would be, if Providence should only leave us to ourselves or (as they commonly say) to our own destruction."[20] Humphreys' language here reflects an exceedingly low estimate of "the people at large"—they were stupid, negligent, dissipated, licentious, and avaricious; clearly, in his view, they could not be trusted with their own government. The image of Humphreys revealed here is important: he saw himself as an eighteenth-century gentleman who was devoting himself to the public service, and it occurred to him as an article of faith that those in government knew better than those governed what was good for them.

Within a few days after writing the letter, Humphreys joined Greene at his headquarters near Morristown only to find that the camp had already broken. The movement of British troops under General Wilhelm Knyphausen, which culminated on 23 June in the skirmish at Springfield, had put Washington and his men in motion. On the twenty-third Knyphausen, with a force of between 5,000 and 6,000 men, met Greene, whose total force numbered between 1,000 and 2,000; Knyphausen was forced to withdraw, but as he did so, he burned down all but four of the fifty dwellings there.[21] Throughout the fighting Humphreys served at Greene's side. He also prepared a detailed report to Washington on the status of the battle at "11 O Clock A.M." at the "Heights near Springfield," on 23 June 1780. It was later that same day that Washington officially appointed Humphreys to his own military family as aide-de-camp. Certainly, the two or three short weeks that Humphreys spent as aide to Nathaniel Greene were the realization of his long-simmering desire to take a truly active role in the Revolution. As Putnam's aide he had been stationed at a considerable distance from the war, but as soon as he joined Greene, and while en route to Washington, he saw immediate action. It was a gratifying step for the young patriot whose energy and ambition seemed, at that point, boundless.

In June 1780, when Humphreys joined Washington's staff, the Commander's military family consisted of Col. Tench Tilghman, Col. Alexander Hamilton, the Marquis de Lafayette, and Col. James McHenry. Sporadically for the next ten years, Humphreys was a welcome member of Washington's military and civilian households. He held an increasingly confidential and professional relationship with the General, one which developed as well into a warm personal friendship. At the time of his appointment as aide-de-camp, Humphreys wrote to his friend Jeremiah Wadsworth, "You see by the dating of my Letter, that I have been honoured with an appointment, my ambition & vanity could hardly prompt me to expect."[22]

Shortly after the battle of Springfield, Washington moved his headquarters to the home of Col. Dey at Preakness, near the Passaic River in New Jersey. He planned to watch the actions of Sir Henry Clinton from that vantage point. Retaking the Tory stronghold of New York was still his objective. The summer, then, was spent in a comfortable, though perhaps somewhat tense, waiting period for the entire military family. Once, when Clinton took 6,000 men to Rhode Island, Washington moved 10,000 into New York, only to return across the Hudson when Clinton returned unexpectedly. The new headquarters were at Tappan, but the old waiting and watching continued.

It was to the house at Tappan in the late summer of 1780 that Major John André, the highly polished aide of Henry Clinton, was brought as a spy after his part as chief British negotiator in the treason of Benedict Arnold was discovered. André was widely admired and given sympathetic treatment by nearly everyone at Washington's headquarters, including David Humphreys.[23] Toward Arnold, however, Humphreys' judgment ran harsh and vindictive. He wrote in a letter (from Passaic Falls, where headquarters had been reestablished) to Jeremiah Wadsworth: "What a scene of horror has displayed itself since I saw you last! Arnold has now become like a twice told tale of infamy—and so let him sink in perdition tho not in oblivion."[24]

Joel Barlow, whom Humphreys had earlier recommended to Greene as a "very great genius," was also on hand for André's execution on 2 October. Later that month Humphreys, Barlow, and others dined together, and after dinner Humphreys talked Barlow into leaving his plan for the "Vision of Columbus" and the completed first book "to read at the headquarters."[25] In that earlier recommendation of 10 April 1780, Humphreys had said:

There is a hopeful Genius . . . in this Town, who is so far gone in Poetry that there is no hope of reclaiming, & making him attentive to any thing else—. . . The person intended, is a young Gentleman by the name of Barlow; who I could wis[h] was introduced to your notice—He is certainly a very great Genius, and has undertaken a work which I am persuaded, will do honor to himself, & his Country, if he is enabled to prosecute it, in the manner he has proposed—It is entitled the Vision of Columbus, and . . . from a sight of the first Book which he has nearly finish'd, I have conceived an exceeding high idea of the performance.[26]

Given Humphreys' high estimate of Barlow's worth as a patriotic poet and the accessibility of Washington, there is little doubt but that Humphreys aided his young friend's career considerably.

Humphreys' "Elegy on Lieutenant de Hart" may well have been written during the late fall of 1780, although the evidence is all internal and does allow for a later composition. The poem is set in autumn, as the first stanza announces, and a footnote to the title describes de Hart as a "Volunteer Aid" to General Wayne, "killed in the attack on the block-house, near Fort Lee, 1780." The "Elegy" contains nine eight-line stanzas; the first and last are in the voice of the poet and frame stanzas two through eight, which are in the lamenting voice of de Hart's sister. The death of a "young warrior"— he was eighteen when he died—continued to be one of the noblest and most moving subjects for Humphreys, and to put the lament into the voice of the dead warrior's sister was to achieve pathos in addition to nobility—or so the poet hoped.

De Hart's sister tells the reader that the young man was shot in the chest while leading a charge, that he looked "ghastly in death":

> "My brother, the pride of the plain,
>   "In vain did the graces adorn;
> "His blossom unfolded in vain,
>   "To die like the blossom of morn." (MW, 29–32)

She addresses war ("Oh war! thou hast wasted our clime"), concluding with a rhetorical question: " 'Alas! was so finish'd a form / Design'd for so early a tomb?' " (MW, 39–40). The poet in the end merged his voice with that of the sister as she calls on "ye heroes" for vengeance:

> "My hero will never return:
> "He died in the dawn of applause,
>   "His country demanded his breath;

"Go, heroes, defend the same cause,
   "Avenge, with your country, his death." (*MW*, 60–64)

Humphreys had arrived again at his favorite theme among the war poems—urging on the country, and the soldiers especially, to greater purpose and perseverance.

In December 1780 Washington's army formed a line from West Point to Morristown, and, to be within easy access of all parts of that line, Washington moved his headquarters to New Windsor. From there, on Christmas night, Colonel Humphreys led a small, ill-fated, expedition into New York, intending to capture either Wilhelm Knyphausen or Sir Henry Clinton. To accompany him on this mission, he took three officers and forty men. His earlier success on two similar missions made him confident despite prohibitive odds against success. No doubt Humphreys also took heart by recalling Washington's surprising success at Trenton on 26 December 1776. The expedition set out in a barge and two whaleboats from Dobbs Ferry, but because of a northwest wind that night, the three boats were blown past the Battery, managing to land finally at Brunswick. Humphreys' extraordinary plan misfired without coming close to a successful conclusion. He led the men back to camp by land on 1 January.[27]

During February and March 1781, Humphreys was traveling in New England, his mission to report on the best way to raise troops. He was back at headquarters in New Windsor on 29 March. His discouraged appraisal of his own personal success as well as the future success of the patriot cause is contained in the letter to Jeremiah Wadsworth (dated 9 April 1781) in which he concluded that "our Reg[ts] will be very weak this campaign."[28]

Only ten days before Humphreys' discouraging letter to Wadsworth, he had written of the action at Guilford Courthouse. Here, too, he sounded disspirited:

There has been an action on the 15th Ins[t] between Gen[l] Greene & Lord Cornwallis, near Guilford Court House in North Carolina—No official account has arrived—few particulars are known—It is certain the engagement has not been decisive, as Cap Singleton who was in the action, & left our Army the day after, one mile & an half from the Enemy, &

reports to Govr Jefferson, that Gen Greene would have offered Battle, the day he left Camp, if it had not proved very rainy—he further adds that our loss was said to be between three & four hundred Kill'd & wounded & that of the Enemy many more, but it appears they remain'd on the field of action.[29]

Perhaps it was with a sense of personal frustration at his failure to capture Knyphausen or Clinton and with a growing discouragement over the prospects of raising troops that the news of Greene's battle with Cornwallis reached Humphreys. The news from Captain Singleton had been sketchy and inconclusive, but Humphreys seems to have revealed his own (and perhaps the first official) attitude toward the battle when he concluded discouragingly that the enemy "remain'd on the field of action." Anxiety for the war effort in general, concern over his own misperceived "failures," and the relative dullness of his current paperwork in Washington's New Windsor headquarters may have conspired to put Humphreys into an extended and uncharacteristic despondency. Fortunately, the direction of the war was about to change for the better, and Humphreys' frustrations would soon be likewise reversed.

In March 1781 Washington and Jean Baptiste Rochambeau, commander of the French army in America, were intent on implementing a plan to retake New York City, although Washington was being urged by Governor Thomas Jefferson and others to bring his troops to Virginia. Late in May summer headquarters were established at Dobbs Ferry, and David Humphreys, who with Tench Tilghman comprised what Washington termed his "small family," settled into a new home but resumed tedious old responsibilities. Surviving letters from May, June, July, and early August reveal that Humphreys' work still concerned the raising of troops and provisions.

On 14 August Washington learned that Admiral François de Grasse was sailing for the Chesapeake with twenty-nine warships and more than 3,000 troops and that he would remain there "for combined operations" until the middle of October, when he would return again to the West Indies. This news determined Washington's course of action: he would temporarily abandon his New York campaign in order to mass the bulk of his forces against Cornwallis in the South. The troops were readied and the movement began on 20

August. By the fourteenth of September, Washington, his troops, and his military family were already in Williamsburg, and by the third week in September the strategy against Cornwallis was in operation. The siege of Yorktown ended on 19 October with the surrender of Lord Cornwallis.

Tench Tilghman was given the responsibility of riding as fast as possible to Philadelphia to convey the happy news of Washington's victory. Washington, however, took an additional ten days to prepare a written report of the affair and then sent David Humphreys to Philadelphia to present to Congress the formal written account and, more dramatically, the surrendered British standards. In his letter to the President of Congress, dated 27–29 October 1781, Washington introduced his young aide, whom by then he had come to regard as his protégé: "My present Dispatches being important I have commited it to the Care of Colo Humphrey One of my Aides De Camp, whom, for his Attention, Fidelity, and good services, I beg leave to recommend to Congress and your Excellency."[30]

Humphreys arrived in Philadelphia on 3 November after being received by citizens rather ceremoniously on his trip northward. A Philadelphia news account of his arrival reported that he was "met on the commons by the City troop of horse, and by them paraded through two or three streets of the city, preceded by the colours of the United States and France to the State House, where he laid the standards at the feet of Congress to the great joy of a numerous concourse of spectators."[31] For his service in presenting the surrendered standards, Congress resolved on 3 November "that an elegant sword be presented in the name of the United States, in Congress Assembled, to Colonel Humphreys. . . ."[32]

Upon Humphreys' return to Yorktown, he was invited to accompany Washington back to Mount Vernon from where, with Martha Washington, they proceeded to Philadelphia to tell Congress of the Commander's plans for the immediate future. They arrived at the capital in mid-November and remained there until the end of March 1782. Washington's arrival had been unannounced and therefore not attended by great ceremony. Shortly afterward, however, there were many great celebrations honoring the Commander and his family. No record of Humphreys' responsibilities, if there were any,

during the nearly four months spent in Philadelphia has survived.
The only evidence of his activities and feelings during this time is
contained in a poem, printed here in its entirety for the first time,
entitled "The Farewell," "Written by a soldier on leaving Philadelphia." There are two manuscript versions of the poem, written,
it appears, in late March.[33] Humphreys prefaced the poem in a letter
to Jeremiah Wadsworth:

> I believe I gave you a ludicrous discription of the Scenes of life in
> Philadelphia when I was at that place [apparently in a letter no longer
> extant] & told you how sick I was of them while there was something else
> to do—The following was wrote an evening or two before I came away,
> for my own amusement. I suppose you will say it is an admirable instance
> (not of Poetry) but of that passion of r[ai]ling at those pleasures we have
> already enjoyed, & to which we are at last forced to bid adieu—You may
> call it what you please, it is neither more nor less than the Map of my
> feelings at the time when I was about bidding farewell to Philadelphia.[34]

If Humphreys' comment about railing at pleasures that have already
run their course can be taken at face value—and this is a debatable
point—the poem assumes the rather uncharacteristic posture of
Romantic self-examination:

> Adieu ye scenes, so gaily form'd to please!
> Ye fatal [festal] days, and nights with rapture fraught;
> Ye joys, that lull us in the lap of ease,
> Unnerve the arm, and chill the daring thought.
>
> Such are the joys that fill thy constant round,
> Oh Philadelphia, 'midst the rage of war!
> Thy pride exults, as thund'ring o'er the ground
> Roll the swift wheels of pleasure's gilded car.[!]
>
> How chang'd, oh beauteous town, thy simple lot,
> For lo! thy sons with alter'd manners gay,
> [(] Thy sapient founder's sober plans forgot [)],
> Change nature's laws, and turn the night to day.
>
> Go then, ye proud, in all the glare of dress,
> Go swell the riot—turn the deaf'ned ear
> To patriot virtue, groaning in distress,

Nor shed for human woe, one tender tear.
[Nor shed for woe the sympathetic tear.]

But can the revels of nocturnal sports,
The charms of music, or the pride of show
Drive hostile navies from your guarded ports
Or shield your country from the barb'rous foe! [?]

Is this a time for feasts of flowing bowls?
[Is this a time for feasts & flowing Bowls]
Or can ye sleep! while yet your country bleeds!
Let other thoughts now rouse your slumb'ring souls,
And other prospects prompt to nobler deeds—[!]

Farewell the soft delights that pleas'd before,
Farewell awhile to beauty's blooming charms;
And hark! the trumpets sound, the cannons roar;
The pulse beats high as glory calls to arms:

Ours be the music of the roaring wind,
The drum sonorous, and the shrill-ton'd fife—
Ours the dread scenes, which charm th'enraptur'd mind,
Wake the bold wish, touch the springs of life.

'Tis ours to claim th'inestimable prize,
Where independence spreads the glorious meed—
Rise then, my country, in one effort rise, [!]
And one campaign shall crown th'immortal deed.

As part of Washington's official family, Humphreys had accompanied the General and his wife to many dinners and social events. The time was spent pleasantly, with little thought given to military affairs.[35] But there certainly was "something else to do," and excessive celebrating was potentially dangerous if Americans—Washington's family included—hoped to maintain the proper military alertness. On the one hand, the poem is typical in that it appeals to patriotic sentiment, but if it is also Romantically confessional, it would be very atypical as well: Humphreys may have been saying that he, too, had been lulled "in the lap of ease" and had his own arm "unnerved." Because of these deadly effects, his "festal" days in Philadelphia were also "fatal," explaining the appropriateness of both words in line two. Of course, no one could know for sure that the war was then all but over, and so it was a cautious Humphreys who may have been trying to sober himself and a jubilant Philadelphia as well, after several months of indulgent high living.

The spring and summer of 1782 appear to have been spent uneventfully for Washington's family in Newburgh. The lynching of Captain Joseph Huddy in mid-April marked the beginning of an eight-month story known as the Huddy-Asgill Affair. Huddy had been executed by a band of twelve Tories led by Captain Richard Lippincott, who believed him to have been involved in the death of a well-known Tory, Philip White. Washington demanded of Sir Henry Clinton that Captain Lippincott be turned over to the American forces for punishment, a demand that Clinton refused. Washington then wrote an order "to choose by lot a [captured] British officer of equal rank . . . to suffer for [the] murder of Capt. Huddy."[36] Nineteen-year-old Charles Asgill, a captain of the guard, was chosen. Asgill's execution was delayed while appeals for mercy were given a chance to circulate. In November Congress ordered Washington to release Asgill, which he did; however, Washington was denounced roundly for being unnecessarily harsh and vindictive in his proposed eye-for-an-eye justice. Afterward, David Humphreys undertook a defense of Washington and published it in the *New-Haven Gazette and Connecticut Magazine* for Thursday, 16 November 1786. The title of the essay was "The conduct of General Washington Respecting the Confinement of Captain Asgill placed in the true Point of Light." On the day of its publication, Humphreys sent a copy to Washington, saying simply, "I have no fear but that the truth will become generally known."[37]

The summer of 1782 was spent pleasantly, with a great deal of Humphreys' time devoted to literary matters. He had ample opportunity to make a full-scale revision of his "Address to the Armies." He brought the poem up to date, urging perseverance in the face of apparent victory. In September he wrote to Nathaniel Greene seeking support in getting subscriptions for Barlow's "great Poetical work," which "by the immense labour and efforts of the Author is now nearly compleated. . . ."[38] Apparently Humphreys did some new writing of his own, too. It is likely, for example, that Sonnet III, "On the Prospect of Peace, in 1783," was written during the last six months of 1782. The poem sounds as if it were an outgrowth of the peace section of the "Address to the Armies," the revision of which he had just been completing. In the opening apostrophe of the quatrain, Peace is asked to "Bring heav'nly balm to heal my country's wounds." The first quintain announces that for too long now the cannon has "insufferably roar'd" and that it is now time to "sheath the wearied sword." The final quintain proclaims that the "voice divine" had bid "th'invaders yield." The final four lines of the poem are held together by the metaphor of a new day, signifying a new era of liberty and independence. What had been "glooms of midnight" have been transformed into "morn's gay prospects": "There, see the dawn of heav'n's great day revealed."

The most important new work that Humphreys apparently wrote during the summer of 1782 is "The Glory of America; Or, Peace Triumphant over War."[39] The poem was printed in Philadelphia in 1783, with Humphreys' authorship poorly hidden by the statement on the title page that the poem was "Printed for the Author, by E. Oswald and D. Humphreys." The attribution to Humphreys, however, depends more on an internal examination of the poem than on this one piece of ambiguous external evidence. "The Glory of America" is a verse oration of 329 lines, written in heroic couplets. It relies heavily on heightened rhetoric and contains a clear division into exordium, narration, and peroration. Moreover, in content and theme the poem is similar to Humphreys' other patriotic verses. The exordium introduces "Columbia's genius," who sings rhapsodically in the opening line of the narration, "Hail, favor'd land! all hail. . . ." The poet praised the land—a "paradise new-risen from the wild"—as well as the "lowing herds" and "sportive flocks." Then, in a series of questions, the poet shifted his tribute to the heroes of the Revolution. Both the rhetorical use of questions and the review of war heroes are typical of Humphreys:

> What gallant leaders exercis'd command?
> What noble vet'rans led the martial band?
> What souls of peerless worth so long have fought?
> And who our happy Independence wrought?
> Declare, O Muse—Their names, their feats review,
> And glad commemorate the virtuous few. (ll. 47–52)

At the head of the list, of course, is Washington, but the poet wrote, as only an intimate could, of the Commander-in-Chief's strong desire to return to Mount Vernon:

> To rural scenes thou may'st again retire,
> What thou so long, so ardent did'st desire;
> Serene thy days shall glide, disquiets cease,
> A blissful life of piety and peace. (ll. 63–66)

Other heroes follow—Greene, Gates, and Putnam: "To such, what vast acknowledgements are due!" The poet gives tribute to "th'illustrious dead" and to "the Gallic King." There is a battle scene, true to Humphreys' sense of the sublime, in which "Death glutted stalks, the thund'ring cannons roar, / And loud rebellow through the distant shore" (ll. 124–25). An impassioned apostrophe to "Deluded Britain!" is followed by an apostrophe to America, which sounds very like Humphreys in its figures of speech and sentiment: "All-favour'd land! fair freedom's choicest seat! / With countless blessings, many a joy replete. / Dear native country! of thy fame I sing—" (ll. 151–53). American justice, industry, agriculture, and science are all hailed, and in the peroration the poet predicted future greatness in poetry. More importantly, he predicted commercial and naval greatness as well:

> Our navy, like a bulwark on the main,
> Appal encroaching tyrants, who may strive,
> Of native rights our country to deprive;
> While our tall ships far distant realms explore,
> And waft their produce here from ev'ry shore. (ll. 313–17)

In several regards "The Glory of America" had Humphreys' unmistakable stamp. The first suggestion of Humphreys is the oratorical—epideictic—structure and the heavy dependence on apostrophes, questions, and exclamations. Second is the poem's thematic movement from praise of the land to praise of the heroes of the Revolution to praise of American justice, agriculture, and science. Of particular significance is the attention to industry and commerce and the need of a navy to defend America's "native rights"—all themes of Humphreys' later work. Although the attribution cannot be made with absolute certainty, the internal evidence argues strongly that Humphreys did write "The Glory of America"; furthermore, it would appear that he wrote it during the summer of 1782.

News of the peace treaty did not reach headquarters, which in August had been relocated to Princeton, until 31 October 1783. In the interim period of about a year's duration, David Humphreys continued routine duties as one of Washington's aides, duties which included inspections of army posts and reports on supplies. In addition to this work, there were new assignments having to do with the conclusion of the war, and Humphreys found himself writing many final reports for Congress and answering many letters for Washington. The trying period of waiting continued, first in Newburgh, then in Princeton, until word of the peace arrived. At that time Humphreys and two others were invited to accompany the Commander into New York and, after that, to Annapolis and Mount Vernon. Washington then moved his military family to West Point, where he made preparations to reoccupy New York.

During November and December 1783, Humphreys answered many letters for Washington. He by then understood the General's mind so well that he easily drafted replies containing friendly praise, a recognition of God's providence, and a faith in the future glory of America. Moreover, he managed to make each letter different from the others, so that it appeared the General was taking a personal interest in each one. Without question Humphreys' letters at this time relieved Washington of a considerable burden and showed him off to best advantage as well. [40]

By 25 November Washington, his staff, and an escort were poised in Harlem for their march into New York. The triumphant and glorious march was made—a moment of dignity, nobility, and great personal gratification for everyone involved. Humphreys may have written Sonnet IV, "On Disbanding the Army," at this time, although it could well have been written at any nostalgic moment thereafter. In this poem, Humphreys gave way to a sentimentality which is dangerously close to the surface in several of his war poems. His apostrophe in this one is to the army: "Ye brave Columbian

bands! a long farewell!" Theirs is a friendship of "suff'rings sweet":
"Ah! never, never more on earth to meet: / Distill'd from gall that
inundates the heart, / What tears from heroes' eyes are seen to start!"
(*MW*, 7–9) Finally, the poet-warrior bade farewell to those "who
fell in fields of gore"; he is consoled, however, by the thought that
soon they will be joined again "on the peaceful shore." This poem,
while motivated by a genuine emotion, never overcomes its sentimentality and is easily the weakest of those written during the
Revolutionary War years.[41]

Washington said goodbye to his officers at Fraunces' Tavern on
4 December, and then, still accompanied by his staff, he set off for
Annapolis, where, on 23 December 1783, flanked by Humphreys
and Tilghman, he officially resigned his commission as Commander-
in-Chief. Washington and his military family were then ready for
their trip to Mount Vernon.

Chapter Three
Favorite

Between 1784 and 1790 David Humphreys received many political and social favors. George Washington recommended him to Congress, thus providing the stimulus for Humphreys' appointment in 1784 as secretary to a European commerce commission. Humphreys served the commission for twenty-one months and became a professional and personal favorite of commissioners Thomas Jefferson and John Adams. When Humphreys returned to America in April 1786, Jefferson and Adams wrote several letters of recommendation, hoping to secure a new congressional appointment for him. This, however, did not occur. Instead, after spending a five-week vacation with the Washington family at Mount Vernon, Humphreys returned home to Connecticut where he was elected to the General Assembly. With the outbreak of Shays' Rebellion Humphreys was honored with the command of a regiment. Still later he accepted Washington's invitation to live permanently at Mount Vernon. In April 1789, when Washington left for New York to become president, Humphreys accompanied him and continued in his customary role as Washington's secretary, personal aide, and trusted advisor. In late 1789 Washington and Jefferson asked Humphreys to undertake a delicate, secret mission in London, Lisbon, and Madrid—the beginning of a diplomatic career that would keep him in European capitals almost exclusively for the next twelve years. Most important to Humphreys' impressive public service was George Washington's great faith in the abilities of his young friend and protégé.

During the years between 1784 and 1790, Humphreys also wrote a great deal of his most important poetry and prose. The poetry included his 1786 "On the Happiness of the United States" and his contribution to the "American Antiquities" (*The Anarchiad*), published originally in the *New-Haven Gazette and Connecticut Magazine*,

October 1786 to September 1787. These plus several shorter poems—new and old—appeared in magazines and newspapers throughout New England and gave to Humphreys a postwar, popular reputation that approached Freneau's or Trumbull's. In prose he wrote the *Life of Putnam* (1787–88), presenting it to the Connecticut Society of the Cincinnati on 4 July 1788. He also began, but never completed, an authorized life of Washington. In late 1788 he produced a play, *The Widow of Malabar,* "imitated" from the French tragedy of Antoine Le Mierre. His literary activity was capped in 1790 with the publication of *Miscellaneous Works.* From a literary standpoint as well as a political, military, and social one, David Humphreys appeared to be one of God's favored people in the 1780s. He was a popularly successful poet, a prominent military figure, an elected politico, and a soon-to-be-recognized diplomat of stature.

Secretary

Washington and his family arrived from Annapolis at Mount Vernon on Christmas Eve 1783. David Humphreys was invited to be with Washington during the homecoming, made doubly festive by the holiday season. Soon after the first of the year, however, Humphreys left for Connecticut with an uncertain future before him. He wanted to continue in the public service, and, because of Washington's unusual request to President Thomas Mifflin that Humphreys receive the special attention of Congress, he had good reason to expect that a position might be forthcoming. Moreover, Mifflin had asked Humphreys in Annapolis to suggest some positions for which he might be qualified. With a government appointment in the offing, Humphreys held back his inquiries into private business. Should Congress have found no position for him, however, Humphreys needed the money Congress owed him in order, as he put it, to enter "some useful tho' humbler walk of life."[1] In either case, Humphreys found himself dependent on Congress.

Humphreys recognized the potentially paralyzing effect of his situation even before he left Mount Vernon early in January and wrote to Washington on the sixth that he was "strongly inclined . . . to continue in some department of the public employment."[2] He further suggested that he might be suitable as Secretary of

Foreign Affairs or in command of a regiment or as secretary to one of the commissions abroad, and, most important, he asked Washington to write a letter recommending him. Washington responded on 14 January with a letter to Congress. He reminded President Mifflin of his offer to Humphreys, who was, he said, "desirous of continuing in the walk of public life." Washington, however, rearranged Humphreys' suggestions, placing the command of a regiment and secretary of an embassy before the possibility of naming him Secretary of Foreign Affairs. Washington explained in his letter that he did not question Humphreys' competency for the last position, only "the propriety of my suggesting it." He added, "For his ability, integrity, punctuality, and sobriety I can fully answer."[3]

Despite his expectations, Humphreys received no appointment through February, March, and April. On 7 May the commission to negotiate treaties of commerce was authorized by Congress, and Adams, Franklin, and Jefferson were named commissioners. On 11 May, Humphreys was summoned to Philadelphia and met with Thomas Jefferson to discuss the position of secretary, although it was not formally offered to him until the seventeenth. As soon as he received the invitation, he wrote a letter of acceptance.

On 18 May Humphreys asked George Washington for several letters of introduction, saying that he needed them by 10 June, when he was planning to leave with Thomas Jefferson for Paris.[4] Early in June, the letters arrived. Of these, only the letters to Franklin and Jefferson and the general certificate are extant.[5] In the letter to Franklin, Washington wrote: "This Gentleman was several years in my family as an Aid de Camp.—His zeal in the cause of his [country], his good sense, prudence, and attach[ment to] me, [have] rendered him dear to me; a[nd I per]suade myself you will find no con[fide]nce you may think proper to rep[ose] in him misplaced.—He possesses [an excellent] heart, good natural & acquir[ed abilities], and sterling integrity [Humphreys' copy erroneously reads *honesty*]—to whi[ch] may be added sobriety, & an obliging disposition[.]"[6] In much the same manner, Washington wrote to Jefferson: "In him you will find a good scholar, natural & acquired abilities, great integrity, and more than a common share of prudence.—I am certain he will abuse no confidence which may be reposed in him—that he will attempt to discharge the duties of his office faithfully—& will make grateful returns for your civilities."[7] In the certificate Washington wrote, "I do hereby certify" that "during the whole course of his [army] service he was actuated by an ardent zeal to promote the public weal. That his bravery and spirit for enterprize were conspicuous on all occasions, and his intelligence and attention to the duties of his office were of singular use to me, obtaining, as they justly merited, my highest regard and confidence." As he was about to depart for Paris in the apprenticeship of a diplomatic career, Humphreys carefully packed the letters written by George Washington, letters which testified, in the most explicit language, to the great faith he placed in the talents of his former aide.

Humphreys sailed for France on 15 July aboard the *Courier de l'Europe* and arrived at L'Orient on 8 August. During the crossing, he wrote a verse letter, "An Epistle to Dr. Dwight," which reflects in "sea-born numbers" his health and cheerfulness. He found "ten thousand little pleasures" aboard the ship—including food, wine, and liquor. Looking into the galley, he observed that the "Fires, not poetic, much good cheer produce." He rejoiced at the companionship on board, "well-bred passengers, discreet and free," remarking particularly on General Kosciuszko, "Our Polish friend, whose name still sounds so hard, / To make it rhyme would puzzle any bard" (*MW,* 213). Humphreys concluded by telling Dwight that though he would travel through Europe, he would "bring home a patriot heart, enlarg'd, improv'd." Humphreys wished to emphasize that his patriot's heart was not in jeopardy.[8]

While Humphreys no doubt thought of this poem as little more than an exercise in friendly wit for an old friend, it is often quite successful as he merged the lightness of his tone and subject matter with an occasional serious thought and maintained all the while a friendly cordiality. The poem's success results from the overall ease— even playfulness—which characterizes it; this fact is surprising because the poem is written in Humphreys' usual heavily rhetorical style. It differs slightly from Humphreys' "Letter to a Young Lady in Boston," in which he demonstrated a capacity, through half the poem at least, to employ the rhetorical style for humorous, mock-epic purposes. The "Epistle" is not a mock epic; rather, it is loosely structured around the "ten thousand little pleasures" contributing to the poet's health and cheerfulness. The result is a light poem, distinguished by its charm and warmth.

When Humphreys arrived in Paris, he was something of a literary celebrity because his "Address to the Armies" had been republished in French and enthusiastically received. His own popularity as a literary figure combined with his official position to earn for Humphreys a welcome reception in French society: he attended the theater, appeared at court, and was invited to dinners and diplomatic functions.

The social and literary position Humphreys enjoyed in the late summer and early fall of 1784 seemed to make him sanguine about America's political future. He wrote to an unidentified correspondent:

I am sorry to find you so ill boding a prophet respecting our federal Union—for me, I cannot but augur much better things of it—that guiding hand which pointed the way thro' darkness & tempest to Independence, will not desert us in the haven of security, or suffer us by our folly to destroy the fairest prospect of happiness which ever fell [to] the lot of humanity—No, no, my dear Sir, this must not, cannot be—the good sense of our Countrymen will ultimately triumph over the combination of prejudice, error, & misinformation; and induce them by a full compliance with the requisitions of Congress to give that weight and respectability to the federal head which are alone wanted to remedy the defects of our Continental Government: It is a consummation devoutly to be wished.[9]

The opinion expressed in this letter, that the Articles of Confederation would survive, is less important than Humphreys' conviction that a strong federal union was necessary.

Little is known of Humphreys' day-to-day activities in Europe. John Adams, however, was able to form a high estimate of him as early as 28 April 1785, for on that date he wrote to Elbridge Gerry that Humphreys' "Genius, Taste, and knowledge are distinguished, and his heart is excellent."[10] By late August 1785, about one year after his arrival in Paris, Abigail Adams was already anticipating Humphreys' expected arrival in London, although he did not actually get there until November. According to Jefferson in a letter to

Monroe (27 January 1786), Humphreys eventually went to London because there was "nothing going on here under the commissions to which he is Secretary, and some little matter there."[11] Humphreys' official responsibilities, then, were not particularly burdensome. In the place of other, more important work, he may well have had considerable opportunity to indulge in literary work, although no certain evidence exists that he wrote anything other than his long poem "On the Happiness of America."

From London on Christmas Eve 1785, Humphreys wrote a letter to John Jay, the Secretary of Foreign Affairs, stating his intention to return home in April unless there was further need of his services. In the same letter he referred for the first time to "Happiness of America," explaining why he wrote it: "The Newspapers of both parties have co-operated to produce a belief throughout the Continent that the United States are on the brink of perdition. To counteract . . . these unfavourable sentiments I have written . . . a Poem of considerable length addressed to the Citizens of the United States calculated to show their superior advantages for happiness over all the rest of mankind, whether considered in a physical, moral, or political point of view. The work is in the press and I shall have the pleasure of transmitting a copy to you as soon as it shall be compleated."[12] "Happiness of America" remained "in the press" in London until spring, shortly before Humphreys' departure; it was reprinted later that year in Hartford.

In his "Preface to the Ninth Edition" of "Happiness of America," Humphreys wrote a more deliberate rationale for the poem. Here he revealed a large historical perspective, one that demanded a commensurately ambitious poetic expression. Recognizing what he viewed as the frightening implications and unanswered questions arising from the still new experiment in democratic government, he showed why Americans should be encouraged about the future. He wrote to inspire, "to dissipate gloomy apprehensions." With nothing less than the "political welfare of the species" apparently hanging in the balance, Humphreys reviewed the "distressing apprehensions" of Americans during the years after the war. In order to assuage the fears of "threatening prospects," Humphreys showed his countrymen their "superior advantages for happiness."

"Happiness of America" is quite different from the "Address to the Armies"; for one thing, it has none of the latter's classical parallels and allusiveness. The less complicated, nonclassical framework of the poem is matched by Humphreys' less insistent use of the sublime. He considered the military theme of the "Address" more noble and dignified and, therefore, more suitable to the sublime. As a result, "Happiness of America" is a less pretentious poem than the "Address," one which makes fewer claims at being high art. The poem went through ten editions from 1786 to 1804, reflecting an even greater contemporary popularity than the "Address" had enjoyed.

In every edition of "Happiness of America" except the last, the poem appeared as a 1,094-line verse essay; in its last edition (*MW*, 1804), however, Humphreys divided it into two poems. Under the title "Happiness of America," he included the first 678 lines of the original poem. The remaining lines became the core of "A Poem on the Future Glory of the United States of America."[13] This sudden division converted "Happiness of America" into Humphreys' most unique poem: its oratorical format became hidden by the apparently deliberate omission of a peroration. Ironically, probably because its conformity to oratorical patterns is not so visible, this is probably the most agreeable of all Humphreys' poems to modern readers.

In its final form in 1804, "Happiness of America" is framed at beginning and end with important national concerns, containing in the middle an easy account of domestic America. The Revolution and the death of heroes are both present in the poem, but they have a relatively minor role. The dominant features of the poem are Humphreys' view of the peace and industry existing in agricultural America, the simple amusements associated with the seasons, the pleasant stories of old warriors, and the loveliness of American women. The poem concludes with an appeal for an ambitious plan of naval and commercial activity—the very task he was involved in when writing the poem.

The exordium is a fourteen-line apostrophe to the "happy people" of America. Humphreys tried to demonstrate why the Americans should find happinesss: they have "Columbia's virgin prime"; they are heirs of "immortal fame"; and they are the "chosen race." The narration which follows is a loosely connected series of nine sections. In the first, the poet dramatically recreated Washington's farewell to his officers while in the last, he appealed for a commercial fleet. America's agricultural present and commercial future were complementary, not conflicting, in Humphreys' vision.

The key middle sections of the narration depict American landscapes and manners, the features of the country which give Americans their singular advantage in the pursuit of happiness. Humphreys said that America was not built by "conquest, blood, or usurpation" but "form'd on freedom's base." He offered reasons for happiness which the Americans, because they are a free and agricultural people, can count. They enjoy the simple pleasures, "the joys of innocence and ease, / Of peace, of health, of temp'rance, toil, and rest." There follows a season by season paean to America, a pastoral lyric in which Humphreys spoke with nostalgic fondness of "wanton bow'rs," and the "pastur'd vale," of "yellow harvests," "Ripe autumn," and "snows surcharg'd." He concluded with a portrait of the farmer and his family enjoying the fruits of their labors.

The poem has a wandering quality which captures an easygoing American tempo, and certainly this is part of the subject of the poem. One entire section of the narration, for example, deals with winter amusements and is, like stories of old warriors, appropriately rambling. In fact, it might be said that Humphreys tried to recreate nothing less than the rhythms, the heartbeat, of life in agrarian America. Humphreys made an effort to write about America as it really was, not under the special circumstances of war, but in peace, and the poem reflects a genuine passion for the simple, virtuous people of the country. The content of "Happiness of America" is, therefore, peculiarly American—more so even than the patriotic "Address to the Armies." In all, the poem was successful because of the hope it reflected as well as for the several dimensions of Americanness that its subject revealed.

Humphreys' literary interests in Europe went beyond his own work. During his three-month stay in London, he made several literary acquaintances, including Edmund Burke and Richard Sheridan. At this time, too, he read *The Rolliad,* the mock-epic satirizing Tory government, which later served as the model for *The Anar-*

chiad.[14] He also attended the theater frequently, noting that he thought French theater superior to English. And from Paris, early in March, he mailed a copy of Dwight's *Conquest of Canaan* and a manuscript copy of Barlow's *Vision of Columbus* to John Adams in the hope that Adams might arrange for their publication. Literary matters clearly occupied a good deal of Humphreys' time for several months before he left for America.

As Humphreys neared the end of his work for the commission, he could look back with satisfaction at his own work—as secretary and poet; moreover, he had made new and influential friends, both European and American. When he left London for Paris, in the middle of February, Humphreys took with him the very best wishes of Abigail and John Adams. Abigail Adams wrote to Thomas Jefferson: "It is with regret, I assure you, Sir, that we part with him. His visit here has given us an opportunity of becoming more acquainted with his real worth and merit, and our friendship for him has risen in proportion to our intimacy." John Adams wrote to John Jay on 9 February: "It would be doing an injustice to the public as well as to this Gentleman if I were to let him return without the best Testimony I can give him, of my entire satisfaction in his conduct, from his first arrival, and without the fullest recommendations of him to Congress." Jefferson, too, wrote to Jay in Humphreys' behalf, bearing testimony to his "ready, able, and faithful discharge of all . . . duties." He also wrote to Humphreys that he hoped "our country may avail themselves of your talents in the public service, and that you may be willing to employ them."[15] Humphreys' performance in Europe had obviously given credence to Washington's letters of introduction.

Politician and Poet: *The Anarchiad*

Upon his return to New York, Humphreys wrote to John Jay saying that he would soon call on him with letters and other information of interest. Explaining his intention to go to Mount Vernon shortly, he said that Congress might reach him there with any new orders. Before visiting Mount Vernon, however, Humphreys traveled to his home in Connecticut, stopping off also in New Haven and Hartford. From Hartford on 5 June he wrote to

Thomas Jefferson that the country had changed a great deal since they had left. He reported that Governor Clinton was said to have become an "Anti-federalist."[16] He went on to note the general discontent he observed in America: "Many people appear to be uneasy and to prognosticate revolutions they hardly know how or why. A scarcity of money is universally complained of. But to judge by the face of the country; by the appearance of ease and plenty which are to be seen every where, one would believe a great portion of the poverty and evils complained of, must be imaginary."[17]

George Washington recorded in his diary on 24 July 1786 that when he returned home that night, Humphreys was there. Humphreys remained at Mount Vernon until the first of September, falling easily into the family's routines. Washington's diary entries reflect that Humphreys accompanied him on visits to the plantations, and that he went to church, made social calls, and dined with the family. In short, he enjoyed the easy familiarity with the Washington family that he had earlier come to expect and enjoy.

On 4 August Humphreys wrote his brother John from Mount Vernon. In that letter he showed some picque at the lack of notice he had been given as a poet by the American public, expressed an interest in running for the Connecticut General Assembly, and spoke deprecatingly about his own lack of resolve regarding Washington's biography. First, reflecting on his two and a half months back in America, he said, "I have found by recent experience as well as by former travelling a great deal of the world, that a poet like a prophet is not without honor except *in his own country.*"[18] It would appear that he had grown accustomed to the polite attention paid him in Paris and London as one of America's leading literary figures; at the very least, he felt somewhat slighted. He went on to express his intention to return to Connecticut early in September, and, he continued, "I have no objection to its being known by my friends who are freemen of your town, that I shall be on the spot and if they should think proper to appoint me one of their representatives I will serve them as such." Finally, he spoke of his opportunity to begin working on a biography of Washington: "Here is a noble work before me, but deterred by the magnitude of the enterprise I have not yet had spirit to resolve upon its execution."

In fact, however, the biography was begun during Humphreys' five-week stay at Mount Vernon. Its history went back to July 1784, to the letter Humphreys wrote to Washington shortly before leaving for Europe. At that time Humphreys had urged Washington to see to the writing of a "true account of the war, at least of your military transactions with it. . . ." On 30 September 1784 he wrote again: "It is the first wish of my heart to see some writer assume the pen, who is capable of placing your actions in the true point of light. . . ."[19]

On 15 January 1785 Humphreys wrote to Washington about the subject once again. This letter reveals particularly well Humphreys' desire to see Washington's part in the Revolution permanently set down: "Such a work by having truth, instruction & public utility for its objects would make the evening of your day more precious in the eyes of future ages, than they have appeared in the midst of glory & conquest in their meridean splendour. If however you should decline the task, & if ever I shall have leisure and opportunity, I shall be strongly tempted to enter on it, more with the design of rescuing the materials from improper hands or from Oblivion, than from an idea of being able to execute it in the manner it ought to be done."[20] In January 1785 no one could have known that Washington's "meridean splendour" was not over, and Humphreys was genuinely concerned, as Washington's friend and admirer, that the General's greatness would not be recorded by either Washington or someone who had seen firsthand his wartime achievements.

On 25 July 1785 Washington finally replied to Humphreys' numerous appeals. In a letter Washington cited his own "defective education" and his "want of time" as factors making him "unfit" to write his "commentaries." He then praised Humphreys' abilities, discernment, and "personal knowledge" and invited him to undertake the job: "I can with great truth add that my house would not only be at your service during the period of your preparing this work but (& without unmeaning compliment I say it) I should be exceedingly happy if you would make it your home. You might have an apartment to yourself, in which you could command your own time, you would be considered and treated as one of the family; & meet with that cordial reception & entertainment which are characteristic of the sincerest friendship."[21] Unfortunately, when Humphreys received this letter, he was still in Europe and could not commit himself. As it happened, however, he was back in America six months later, and two months after that he was at Mount Vernon.

When Humphreys arrived at Mount Vernon in mid-July 1786, the much-discussed biography was certainly on the minds of both guest and host. The very build-up of the project, combining with his own insistence for two years past that the biography be written, might account for the fact that he had not "spirit enough to resolve upon its execution." Moreover, Humphreys may very well have found that he needed the five weeks at Mount Vernon simply to readjust to America after spending twenty-one months abroad and to shore up his resources for a future which was not then very well defined. Given these circumstances, it is rather surprising to find that Humphreys actually did begin his life of Washington during the last three weeks of August 1786.[22]

Unfortunately, the manuscript of Humphreys' life of Washington is hardly more than a fragment. After several pages of handwritten introduction, there are only a few pages of biography. On pages two and three Humphreys asserted that he had begun the work only because Washington thought him "more competent in several respects to the execution of the task than any other." His intention, he said, was "to employ my pen in preserving such circumstances . . . relative to himself & the public transactions in which he was concerned, as have come to my knowledge."

The latest full-dress biography of Washington, James Thomas Flexner's four-volume study, points out that Humphreys' fragment was never consulted by earlier biographers. Flexner says that in at least one instance Humphreys, with the authority of Washington behind him, provided key information on a previously disputed aspect of Washington's life. According to Flexner, Washington's early education, a subject of much debate by scholars, is treated definitively by Humphreys, who wrote that Washington's early education "was principally conducted by a private tutor." Humphreys' manuscript is a solid piece of "new" evidence, never before brought to bear on the subject.[23] Given this promising start, it is the more regrettable that the work was never completed.

In a letter to Mathew Carey dated from Mount Vernon on 1 September 1786, Humphreys referred to some enclosed manuscripts—not identified—which he imagined would be "novel & interesting" to Carey's readers in the *American Museum.*[24] In March 1788 Carey devoted the entire poetry section of the magazine to Humphreys. Of the seven poems appearing, probably some of the ones referred to in the letter of September 1786, six were reprints: "Elegy on Lt. de Hart," the epitaph for Scammel, "The Genius of America," "Ode to Laura," "Song," and "The Monkey Who Shaved Himself and His Friends." The remaining poem, "Anacreontic," appears to have been printed there for the first time. Dating the composition of the last two poems is difficult. It is unlikely, for example, that Humphreys wrote any new poetry during the summer of 1786; his crowded vacation schedule and the aborted biography argue against this. The best speculation is that both new poems were written either in Paris or London between July 1784 and April 1786. If this dating is correct, Humphreys probably enclosed them with his letter to Carey, thus accounting for his calling them "novel." In all likelihood he also enclosed the de Hart elegy and the epitaph for Scammel. It is a fair bet that he also enclosed the "Ode to Laura," which had appeared on 6 July 1786, unsigned, in the *New-Haven Gazette and Connecticut Magazine* as "An Ode (Never before printed)."[25] "The Genius of America" was not written until 1787, appearing on 25 January as the fifth number of "American Antiquities"; the "Song," later retitled "The Shepherd: A Song," appeared for the first time on 20 September 1787 in the *New-Haven Gazette.*[26] The exact titles he sent, however, are less important than the fact that he sent any at all. Humphreys' genuine interest in poetry had not abated.

The four poems appearing in the *American Museum* for March 1788, not already discussed here, are the "Ode to Laura," "Song," "Anacreontic," and "The Monkey Who Shaved Himself and His Friends."[27] "The Monkey" is a thirty-eight-line fable, probably written in Europe and revised for publication in the *Connecticut Courant,* 26 February 1787. It is written in four stanzas plus an appended moral and is about a monkey owned by a barber: "And all he saw the barber do, / He mimic'd straight, and did it too"

(*MW*, p. 227). Once, while the barber was out, the monkey shaved first the cat, then the dog, and finally himself. The cat and dog ran off bleeding while the monkey found himself cut "from ear to ear." The moral:

> Who cannot write, yet handle pens,
> Are apt to hurt themselves and friends.
> Though others use them well, yet fools
> Should never meddle with edge tools. (*MW*, p. 228)

The poem's criticism of poor poets is as sharp as the razor and, though a minor work, it stands as one of Humphreys' better performances. The poem does not take itself seriously.

"An Ode Addressed to Laura," on the other hand, has been customarily viewed as a poem that does take itself seriously. Leon Howard, for example, concluded that it was written with "ungraceful pomposity."[28] William K. Bottorff, however, has more recently suggested that the poem is a satire, a mock-serious love poem: "An intentional hyperbole, the poem is rather successful in its irony. It is even a mildly acute parody of the *carpe diem* motif. . . ."[29] Composed of six six-line stanzas, the poem enumerates Laura's charms of "motion, figure, face"; the bee can find no sweeter flower than the "rose-bud of thy lips." When she speaks, the accents "musically roll." The purity of her "snow-white" breast bespeaks the purity of her soul. As the speaker gazes at her charms, he dreams of "halcyon days" when her blue eyes gazed back at him. His "love-sick fancy" dwells on her kisses as he dreams of "intermingling soul with soul." Bottorff suggests that the girl addressed is withholding her favors and that she assumes an attitude which evokes from the poet a certain playful exaggeration, what Bottorff terms a "mocking rebuke." In all, the poem may well be the satiric expression Bottorff argues for, a successful *vers de société*.

Of the two remaining poems, the "Anacreontic," which Humphreys later preferred to call "An Impromptu," contains little of interest, although he did demonstrate some facility with the acrostic form. "The Shepherd: A Song" is a translation of a French ballad. The first of the poems is addressed to a young lady, Martha Redwood, who was about to leave for Europe but who wished, before she left, to have a few lines written by Humphreys. This information, supplied by Humphreys in a note to the poem, plus the fact that he later called it "An Impromptu," suggests that Humphreys wrote the lines on demand, perhaps even while the lady waited. If viewed from this standpoint, the cleverness of the poem appears rather impressive. Like the "Anacreontic," the ballad is also uncharacteristic of Humphreys. It is the only ballad he ever wrote, and the only poem in which a shepherd appears. "The Shepherd" is a translation, but Humphreys' selection of it was deliberate and may indicate the bent of his mind at the time it was written; no biographical analogues are known, however. The poem is about a shepherd, his mother, and his sweetheart, concluding with the shepherd's decision to ask for his sweetheart's hand.

Humphreys claimed in a note to "Mount-Vernon: An Ode" to have written that poem in August 1786, while he was still visiting with the Washington family. In all likelihood, however, he only began the poem then and finished it early in September. On 24 September he wrote to Washington from Hartford: "For myself, having wrote a poem expressive of the satisfaction, I experienced in my residence there [Mount Vernon] & having since been told by some better judges than myself, it is not destitute of merit; I take the liberty of offering a Copy & wish it may be acceptable to my amiable & dear friends under your roof." On 22 October Washington replied that the poem "appears pretty in my eye, & has sentiments & elegance which must . . . render it pleasant to others."[30] Judging from the number of times it was reprinted in the next fifteen years, the poem appears, as Washington had predicted, to have enjoyed a considerable popular success.

The poem shows Washington at the end of the war retiring to Mount Vernon, where the warrior turned his hand to "works of peace." Humphreys asserted—perhaps with more pride than accuracy—that his responsibility, once "return'd from Europe's courts," was "To share his [Washington's] thoughts, partake his sports, / And sooth his partial ear" (*MW*, p. 224). Washington enjoyed elevated conversation and the beautiful passing of seasons at Mount Vernon, but his peace was disturbed because he saw growing licentiousness and rampant anarchy among the people. The poem ends on a hopeful note, with Washington saying that he still had faith in providence, a faith that made his skies "lovelier," his "prospects brighter," and his flowers "fairer."

The poem contains Humphreys' familiar rhetorical flourishes, but it is most significant for its rather early expressions of fear over the popular insurrections in Massachusetts, which began in late August and came to be known as Shays' Rebellion. Once again Humphreys demonstrated that to him political sentiments were suitable for poetic expression.

On or about the first of September 1786, Humphreys left Mount Vernon for Derby and shortly after was elected to the Connecticut Assembly, which sat during October and November in New Haven. His first letter to Washington was to announce his election and to say that politics in New England wore an "unpleasing . . . aspect," and that there was a "state of confusion in Massachusetts."[31] The references, of course, are to Shays' Rebellion, which began on 31 August, when an armed force kept the court in Northampton from sitting. During the postwar depression, many on the western frontier in Massachusetts were unable to pay debts in specie, as they were required by law to do. This inability resulted in many foreclosures and a widespread discontent. Various acts of violence erupted under the leadership of Daniel Shays, but no federal troops existed to suppress the rebellion. When a federal arsenal was threatened, however, on 26 September, Congress acted, authorizing the levy of 1,300 troops for the ostensible reason of protecting the frontiers against the Indians. By 1 November Humphreys had been put in command of a regiment and wrote to Washington that "Government is prostrated in the dust." Nothing, he said, "but a good Providence can extricate us from our present difficulties & prevent some terrible convulsion."[32]

Frustrated and angry, Washington replied: "But for God's sake tell me what is the cause of all these commotions: do they proceed from licentiousness, British influence disseminated by the tories, or real grievances which admit of redress? If the latter, why were they delayed 'till the public mind had become so agitated? If the former why are not the powers of Government tried at once?"[33] On 9 November Humphreys answered "that there is a licentious spirit prevailing among many of the people, a levelling principle." Nine days earlier he had written to Benjamin Franklin to say that the political situation had deteriorated in the Eastern states. To resolve the turmoil, however, "some of us [have] spoken & wrote, reasoned & ridiculed in conversation & in print as much as lay in our power."[34]

This is Humphreys' first known reference, albeit an oblique one, to *The Anarchiad,* the first number of which had appeared on 26 October in the *New-Haven Gazette and Connecticut Magazine.* To Washington on 16 November, two weeks after the second number had been printed, Humphreys made a more direct reference: "I would have sent you several of the late papers . . . , which contained performances by Mr. Trumbull, Mr. Barlow, & myself [note the omission here of Lemuel Hopkins], in a style and manner, I believe somewhat superior to common newspaper publications: but the demand has been so uncommonly great for those papers that there is not a single one to be obtained. In some instances the force of ridicule has been found of more efficacy than the force of argument, against the Anti-federalists & Advocates for Mobs. . . ."[35]

The Anarchiad: A Poem on the Restoration of Chaos and Substantial Night appeared in twelve issues of the *New-Haven Gazette* from 26 October 1786 to 13 September 1787. David Humphreys, Lemuel Hopkins, John Trumbull, and Joel Barlow collaborated, but published the numbers anonymously, creating the impression that the entire "epic" had been written by some hitherto unknown American Homer. The speaker of the introductory prose note to No. I pretended to have found the ancient epic poem in its entirety while he was engaged, as a member of a society of critics and antiquarians, in excavations. He was astonished that the author of the ancient epic could have reflected so perfectly contemporary events in New England. A short poetic fragment was also printed as part of No. I, introducing the figure of Chaos, who "asserts his sway" over Massachusetts. The speaker saw below him Shays and Shattuck with their mobs and concluded:

> Thy constitution, Chaos, is restor'd;
> Law sinks before thy uncreating word;
> Thy hand unbars th'unfathom'd gulf of fate,
> And deep in darkness 'whelms the new-born state.[36]

The Connecticut or Hartford Wits, as they began to be known at this time, published eleven more numbers of "American Antiquities" at irregular intervals, using speeches, soliloquies, songs, heroic games, and visions of the underworld to frame their mock heroic satires.

Authorship of individual numbers, with the single exception of No. V, which David Humphreys later reprinted under his own name, has never been established.[37] Corroborative evidence for attributions is scant and determinations based solely on stylistic analyses, regardless of how suggestive they may be, must remain conjectural. However, some hard evidence does exist, and this, taken with a stylistic examination, provides clues enough for one to draw a number of supported conclusions about the extent of David Humphreys' contribution to *The Anarchiad.* These conclusions are printed here for the first time.

In letters to George Washington dated from New Haven on 16 November 1786 and 20 January 1787, Humphreys mentioned himself, Trumbull, and Barlow as the authors of some "performances" that he believed "somewhat superior to common newspaper publications." In the 20 January letter he said that the *three* of them had "written a good number of pieces in prose & verse on poetical subjects."[38] Humphreys' omission of Hopkins's name from both letters argues that Hopkins had not by then contributed. More to the point, it implies that Hopkins had not originated the plan, thus adding more weight to the theory that Humphreys had. If the omission of Hopkins's name from both letters is significant in this way, it means, at the very least, that Hopkins could not have written any of the first five numbers. (The first four were published before 20 January, and the fifth, dated 25 January, is Humphreys' "The Genius of America.")

The elimination of Hopkins as originator makes Humphreys a likely candidate for authorship of No. I, although a stylistic examination is here inconclusive. No. II has one section which is definitely written in Humphreys' style. In this number Anarch claims Massachusetts and Rhode Island for his own. The verse begins with an Homeric listing of the people who were most faithful to Chaos. The forty-two lines which follow are divided into seven irregular stanzas of heroic couplets. The first four stanzas contain not a single apostrophe, interrogation, or exclamation; neither do the final two stanzas. Stanza five, however, is crammed with all three, suggesting that it, at least, may have been written by Humphreys. With its extraordinary dependence on strong figures, the following stanza sounds very much like Humphreys:

> Why sleep'st thou, *Blacklegs,* child of knavery, why?
> Seest thou, blest Wronghead, helpless how we lie?
> And where is Wimble, earliest squib of fame!
> Your tongue and pens must wake the factious flame!
> And thou, poor Quack, behold thy efforts fail;
> Could one address thy o'erstrain'd wits exhale?
> Wake, scribble, print; arouse thee from thy den,
> And raise conventions with thy blust'ring pen! (Riggs, 10)

The decidedly oratorical quality of these lines as well as their poetic excesses argue that if Humphreys did not write them, one of the others had suddenly fallen into his style.

Humphreys was almost certainly responsible for the prose introduction to No. III (28 December 1786), "Extracts from 'The Anarchiad,' on Paper Money." The author and his confederates "are conscious that the manuscripts from which they have already given specimens . . . , *contain performances in poetry and prose of a very different complexion from those which commonly appear in American newspapers*" (italics added). Humphreys had earlier written about *The Anarchiad* on 16 November to George Washington, using the same language: "I would have sent you several of the late papers . . . , which *contained performances* by Mr. Trumbull, Mr. Barlow, & myself, in a style and manner, I believe *somewhat superior to common newspaper publications* . . ." (italics added). In addition to this similarity of idea and language, there is a Humphreys-like disclaimer about the relative merits of the poem: "While they [the society of critics and antiquarians] publicly disclaim all title to any merit in these productions . . . , they would advise the several printers on the continent to peruse them attentively, and to publish at least such pieces as may be applicable to their particular States." No. III, thus far, sounds like Humphreys.

The verse in No. III contains a very telling stylistic idiosyncrasy: an inordinate fondness for beginning stanzas of heightened rhetoric with *hail!* No. III is only five stanzas long, but the first begins, "Hail! fav'rite State" and the fourth, "Hail! realm of rogues, renown'd for fraud and guile, / All hail!" (Riggs, 14, 16). In almost every one of his important poems, Humphreys began stanzas in a similar fashion, as in the following examples: "Address to the Armies": "Hail, heav'n-born Peace!"; "On the Happiness of America": "Hail agriculture!"; "On the Future Glory of the United States of America": "Columbia, hail!"; "On the Love of Country": "Hail *sacred Love of Country!*" Humphreys underscored his fondness for this type of opening in "On the Industry of the United States of America," where he began three stanzas with *hail:* "Hail favour'd state!" (almost identical to the opening of No. III); "Hail, model of free states!"; and finally:

> Then hail for us, ye transatlantic scenes,
> Soul-soothing dwellings! sight-refreshing greens!
> And chiefly hail, thou state! where virtue reigns,
> And peace and plenty crown the cultur'd plains. (*MW*, 459–62)

Furthermore, it is significant that the only other instance in *The Anarchiad* of a stanza beginning with the word *hail* is in No. V, Humphreys' "The Genius of America": "Hail! ye first bounding ships. . . ." The cumulative evidence leaves little room for doubting Humphreys' authorship of No. III.

Even more certainly, "American Antiquities" No. IV was written by Humphreys. Stanza two is adapted, with obvious good humor, from stanza thirteen of "Happiness of America":

> Thrice happy race! how blest were freedom's heirs,
> Blest if they knew what happiness is theirs,
> Blest if they knew to them alone 'tis given,
> To know no sov'reign but the law and heav'n!
> ("Happiness of America," *MW*, 131–34)
> Thrice happy race! how blest are discord's heirs!
> Blest while they know what anarchy is theirs;
> Blest while they feel to them alone 'tis given
> To know no sovereign, neither law nor Heaven.
> (Riggs, 18–19)

Further suggesting Humphreys is the long debate in No. IV between Anarch and Great Hesper. The speech of Hesper, the voice of patriotic Columbia, is heavy with apostrophes, exclamations, and interrogations, and thus bears the unmistakable stamp of Humphreys:

> "Where is the spirit of bold freedom fled?
> Dead are my warriors; all my sages dead?
> Is there, Columbia, bending o'er her grave,
> No eye to pity, and no arm to save?
>
> Sister of Freedom! heaven's imperial child!
> Serenely stern, beneficently mild,
> Blest Independence! rouse my sons to fame,
> Inspire their bosoms with thy sacred flame!
> Teach, ere too late, their blood-bought rights to prize,
> Bid other GREENES and WASHINGTONS arise!
> Teach those who suffer'd for their country's good,
> Who strove for freedom, and who toil'd in blood,
> Once more, in arms, to make the glorious stand,
> And bravely die, or save their natal land. (Riggs, 23)

These lines are not only too dependent on the strong figures, but they also contain the patriotic intensity and enthusiastic excesses that further recall Humphreys. In addition, the evocation of Greene and Washington, typographically accented, is very much consistent with the military mind of Humphreys, his sense of dignity, and his great regard for both men. In all, Humphreys' authorship of No. IV is very likely.

No. V, "The Genius of America," is Humphreys', and he later reprinted the poem under his own name. It was advertised in the *New-Haven Gazette* as among the "miscellaneous papers" found in the same location with *The Anarchiad*. A prose note containing the nucleus of Humphreys' thinking in "Happiness of America" preceded it: "If Americans could be taught to revere themselves; if they could be made to realize their consequence . . . , so far from being desperate in their situation, . . . [they] might be considered as the peculiar favorites of heaven." The poem itself concerns the birth of

a "mighty empire" where "heavenly light" would finally beam down
on a country of heathen Indians. The speaker sees a war followed
by a blissful peace, and the poem ends with a rhetorical question
as the speaker wonders if "discord" will destroy the people's hard-
fought and well-earned happiness.

Numbers VI, VII, and VIII contain no evidence of having been
written by Humphreys. No. IX, however, probably was; it is the
natural conclusion to No. IV. In No. IV the reader is told that the
"issue of this astonishing conflict" (i.e., the debate between Anarch
and Great Hesper) was unknown, although "we have reason to
conjecture that the combat ended with some disadvantage to the old
Anarch." The story of this combat is continued in No. IX, which
begins with the "situation and soliloquy of Anarch, after [he had
been] vanquished, in single combat by Hesper." This relationship
between numbers IV and IX, plus stylistic similarities of the two,
indicate that Humphreys was most likely responsible for the latter
as well as the former.

No. IX opens with Anarch venting "loud curses" that sound very
much like Humphreys:

> Oh, rage! oh, torture! limbs and armor riven,
> On earth an exile, and the scorn of heaven!
> Robb'd of a world, by lying fates bestow'd,
> Hesper victorious! I a vanquish'd god!
> Gape wide, profoundest hell! in Stygian flame
> Hide your lost Anarch from undying shame!
>
>
> He spoke!   (Riggs, 49)

Night, Anarch's mother, offers consolation to her son by contrasting
Columbia's early days to the days of "confusion" and "eclipse" that
would come. By contriving this situation Humphreys was able to
employ one of his favorite techniques, the review of Revolutionary
War heroes. Moreover, Night speaks with such enthusiastic patriotism that it is impossible not to detect Humphreys' voice in the
not-too-distant background. She says that American soldiers fought,
"while sad Columbia bled, / To save one central region, and restore /

Each glorious exile to his natal shore" (Riggs, 50). The last two lines seem to be a slightly remodeled version of those he had written earlier in No. IV: "Once more, in arms, to make the glorious stand, / And bravely die, or save their natal land" (Riggs, 23). And at the end of her speech to Anarch, Night launches into an emotional and rhetorical peroration that sounds once again very much like Humphreys:

> Rise, then, my son! the frowns of fate to dare;
> Blest with such aid, shall Anarch's soul despair?
> Hark! how my heroes to the field invite,
> Go, more victorious in thy mother's might[.] (Riggs, 53)

All told, the extensive use of heightened rhetoric combines as evidence with Humphreys' telling technique of calling up in review Columbia's past glories and the fact that the subject of No. IX is directly related to No. IV to argue that Humphreys was responsible for No. IX.

"American Antiquities," No. X is a direct address to the members of the Constitutional Convention; it was printed on 24 May 1787, the eve of the seating of the delegates. Its subject, advertised to have been excerpted from Book XXIV of *The Anarchiad,* was an eleventh-hour patriotic speech made by Hesper to his "principal counselors and sages, whom he had convened at Philadelphia." Because of its timing and the directness of its appeal, this number is the climax of the series. Here Hesper makes his last impassioned defense of Columbia.

After receiving the attention of his counselors in a large assembly, Hesper asks them a series of questions, as Humphreys was wont to do, about the future of their country, trying to shame them into not deserting God's unfinished plan. He then directs his listeners to recall—in the Humphreys manner—the heroes of their race: "Go search the field of death, where heroes lost, / In graves obscure, can tell what freedom cost" (Riggs, 55). These lines, in turn, recall the following ones from Humphreys' epilogue to Racine's *Athaliah:* "Heav'ns!—what the price those rights confirm'd have cost, / What treasures lavish'd, and what heroes lost?" (*MW* [1790], 180). Then, just as Humphreys had done in the "Address to the Armies," the

poet of No. X recalled some of the same dead war heroes to honor:
Laurens, Warren, and Mercer: "This hateful truth still aggravates
their pain, / *In vain they conquer'd! and they bled in vain!*" (Riggs,
57). In the epilogue to *Athaliah* Humphreys, recalling the same
heroes, says: "And yet I hear those forms, from many a plain. /
Exulting cry, '*WE HAVE NOT BLED IN VAIN!*' " (*MW* [1790],
180).

Such emotionalism attached to military subjects from the Revolution is very reminiscent of Humphreys in style and content. Just
as significant for an attribution are the language parallels in No.
X and in the poem that Humphreys later published under his own
name, the epilogue to Racine's *Athaliah*. In all, then, if one judges
from the gravity of Hesper's tone throughout, the mixture of rhetoric
and emotionalism, the excessive reliance on exclamation and interrogation, the poet's particular use of the Revolution to spark patriotic
spirit, the denunciation of Europe, and the parallel lines that turn
up again in Humphreys' epilogue to *Athaliah,* the conclusion must
be that Humphreys was, indeed, the author of No. X. This was the
last of the series that Humphreys wrote as there is little or no
evidence in Nos. XI or XII that is suggestive of his work.

To sum up, one can see rather clearly Humphreys' hand at work
in numbers III, IV, V, IX, and X. In addition, assuming, as there
is some reason to do, that the entire series was Humphreys' brain-
child, it is probable that he wrote at least part of No. I. Finally,
there is some stylistic evidence that he may have written at least
one stanza in No. II. These attributions do rely heavily—though
not exclusively—on stylistic analysis, which is always elusive and
tricky, but if substantially correct, they make it possible to conclude
that Humphreys was the single most important contributor to *The
Anarchiad.*

Humphreys spent a large part of the winter of 1786–87 in Hartford where, because of its location in central Connecticut, the men
of his regiment were to assemble. Here he received a letter from
George Washington, dated 26 December, in which Washington
lost patience with the rebels: "What gracious God, is Man! that
there should be such inconsistency & perfidiousness in his conduct?
It is but the other day that we were shedding our blood to obtain

the Constitutions under which we now live. Constitutions of our own choice & making & now we are unsheathing the sword to overturn them."[39] On the same day that Washington wrote these lines, Daniel Shays marched on the Springfield arsenal with 1,200 men.

Humphreys' regiment was not ordered into Springfield until mid-February. On 20 January he was in New Haven and left on 3 February for Hartford from where, with his regiment, he proceeded to Springfield. On 20 January he wrote a long response to Washington's emotional outburst of the twenty-sixth. In it he commented on the weakness of the Articles of Confederation: "We may have found what forms we please, but without co-ertion, they are idle as the wind." He was afraid that the Philadelphia convention might be dominated by Antifederalists, who would provide the country with a still less efficient federal government than it had before. He advised Washington not to attend the convention, saying, "We are already nearly ruined by believing that the Citizens of the United States were better than the rest of the world; and that they could be managed in Society without compulsion."[40] These pessimistic sentiments were evoked in some measure by Washington's own emotionalism, but, given the political upheavals of the time and his own state of military preparedness, his remarks are understandable, if not forgivable.

When Humphreys' regiment was finally ordered to Springfield, the rebellion was all but completely suppressed. Humphreys reported to Washington from there on 28 February that although "the spirit of Rebellion does not seem to be absolutely broken yet it is to be presumed with prudence and perseverance it may be utterly subdued."[41] Shays and the others were unable to withstand General Benjamin Lincoln's attack on them at Springfield on 27 January and his follow-up pursuit through the first week of February. By the time Humphreys and his regiment arrived, the insurrection was virtually crushed. They saw no action at all and within three months were disbanded.

In mid-March Humphreys received a collection of anecdotes from Dr. Albigence Waldo, a former army surgeon, on the life and character of Israel Putnam. In his note of thanks to Waldo, Humphreys said that he hoped someday to have enough leisure to do justice to the subject.

On the first of May Humphreys left New Haven for Philadelphia, where he was to attend the general meeting of the Society of the Cincinnati. Outside Philadelphia he met with Washington and together they entered the city. Washington had decided to attend the Constitutional Convention, despite the pessimistic anticipations he may have shared in some degree with Humphreys. He had heeded Humphreys' advice, however, about attending the general meeting of the Cincinnati, too, for to have spurned that meeting while attending the other would have been a grave offense to the officers of the Revolution. After the short reunion with Washington and the general meeting, Humphreys returned to Connecticut.

There is little documentary evidence indicating Humphreys' activities during the summer of 1787, although he did travel a bit in New England. It is easier to trace his literary career. In June Humphreys' parody "Epithalamium" was published for the first time in the *American Museum.* Since there is no evidence for dating its composition, one might surmise that it was written between September 1786, when the last group of poems had been mailed to Carey, and early 1787. At that time, however, Humphreys was increasingly concerned with political matters and *The Anarchiad* thus making it a better bet that the poem was written between August 1785 and April 1786, while he was in England. Regardless of the date of composition, the "Epithalamium" stands as Humphreys' most elaborate parody. In fact, the parody was so close to its original, Dryden's "Alexander's Feast," that both poems appeared in parallel columns in order to highlight the humorous effects.

Also during the summer of 1787 Humphreys lost both parents, his mother on 29 July and his father on 2 September. Strangely, there is no correspondence extant between Humphreys and his parents, nothing to suggest the relationship he enjoyed with them, either before he entered Yale at age fifteen or afterward. One or both of their deaths may have motivated his Sonnet V, "On Life," for the poem is as much about death as life. Its theme is the transitoriness of time and it contains several images which emphasize the similarities between consciousness, sleep, and the "phantom, life," all the while recognizing the imminence of "th'eternal deep!" The final quintain contains similar images, this time phrased as "moon-light vision's airy shade." The poem concludes in a familiar enough paradox: "true life begins at death." It seems natural that Humphreys, whose father was fifty-four years in the ministry, would turn at the death of his parents to this type of standard Christian consolation.

Humphreys' personal sadness was matched by his continued discouragement over the political situation. He concluded a letter to Alexander Hamilton on 1 September with comments that reflected his deep fears for the country's future: "I leave you now . . . to reflect how ripe we are for the most mad & ruinous projects . . . , especially when . . . we take into consideration how thoroughly the patriotic part of the Community . . . are discouraged with the present System & irritated at the popular Demogogues. . . . Thence apprehensions are formed, that tho' the measures proposed by the convention, may not be equal to the wishes of the most enlightened & virtuous; yet that they will be too high-toned to be adopted by our popular Assemblies."[42] He saw little reason for hope, although he thought it possible that a union of talented and honest supporters of a strong federal government might yet "make the Revolution a blessing instead of a curse."

After the burial of his father, Humphreys began to think again about his delayed trip to Mount Vernon. He wrote to Washington on 28 September that he had been "favourably disappointed & highly pleased" with the published Proceedings of the Convention and that there was nothing left to interfere with the planned visit. "I flatter myself," he said, that "we shall enjoy in the bosom of your family such hours of domestic satisfaction, as I recollect we have experienced formerly at Mount Vernon. I am in full hopes of being on the spot this year to do ample justice to the Christmas Pye."[43] Washington replied that he was very pleased to hear that Humphreys would soon be arriving, saying that "the invitation was not less sincere than the reception will be cordial."[44] In late October Humphreys arrived at Mount Vernon.

Mount Vernon

David Humphreys lived as a member of the Washington family for the next seventeen months and then accompanied the President-Elect to New York, where he stayed on as secretary for another four months. Washington valued the advice and assistance of his former aide, but he also valued him as a friend. Humphreys fit into the family easily, joining Tobias Lear, the children's tutor and secretary to the General, as the only other permanent member of the household.

During the time Humphreys spent at Mount Vernon, he was engaged in writing a play "imitated from the French of M. Le Mierre": *The Widow of Malabar; or, The Tyranny of Custom*. In its published form (*MW*, 1790) the play was preceded by a dedicatory letter to John Trumbull. In the letter Humphreys said that the play had met with "extraordinary success" in its May 1790 production and that the inscription of the play to Trumbull is explained by their being "jointly concerned in writing the Prologue and Epilogue." More important to Humphreys than Trumbull's small written contribution to *The Widow of Malabar* was the "familiarity of genius," "congeniality of soul," and the "indissoluble friendship" that existed between them. These he acknowledged in his open letter to Trumbull. At the same time, he succinctly stated the attitude of the Wits toward the role of poetry, especially during periods of political upheaval: "We shall not be accused of having neglected real business for poetical recreations. Had not the tumultuous scenes, which commenced with the late war, separated our little society, we might have innocently indulged ourselves considerably more in literary speculations than the circumstances have since permitted." Humphreys revealed here the clear distinction the Wits saw between "real business" and "poetical recreations," underscoring the fact that he saw his own poetry as an avocation, though one with a social function. Poetry itself was meant first to instruct, then to delight, and, although it was impossible to separate delight from instruction in any given work, the division was a well-established and traditional poetic priority in the 1780s. Humphreys saw that his chief responsibility was to perform a service for the "real" world, to be employed by his country in whatever capacity his talents would permit. Poetry, despite its instructional value, was not his principal employment, only an allied vehicle through which he could promote public virtue.

Presumably *The Widow of Malabar* was to Humphreys the type of literary speculation that would have received more of his attention had the country not called. Even here, however, the work has a social function—a moral purpose. It is about the cruelty of the Hindu custom of sacrificing a widow after her husband's death. By choosing to "imitate" it, rather than some other play, Humphreys suggested his own approbation of the play's theme, which supports principles of human dignity. There is no political impact in the play, which makes it somewhat unusual for Humphreys, but it is clearly concerned with a serious social problem. By espousing human rights for women, the play instructs.

Humphreys had spent some eighty lines on the "blooming daughters of the western world" in "Happiness of America," and he saw in Le Mierre's play an opportunity to contrast the oppressive East with the free West. In the prologue he offered the following instructions to American women:

> Yet when o'er foreign woes ye shed a tear,
> And find your bliss by contrast still more dear;
> With humble joy adore th'almighty hand,
> Which fix'd your birth in this auspicious land! (*MW*, 1790, 229)

Despite its concern for women's rights, the play fails, largely because it is overladen with situational irony. The widow, for example, is brought to her own funeral pyre by an unwilling young priest— who turns out to be her brother. And the French general, who arrives at the last minute to save her, turns out to be the suitor of her youth, whom her father had forbidden her to marry. The play does contain moments of genuine pathos, because notwithstanding the obvious injustice of the situation, the widow herself prefers to die what she considers an honorable death. Her plight and consequent decision evoke pity, compassion, and admiration. And, although there are many good arguments offered against the custom that is about to claim her life, the duplicity of the governor and high priest, as well as the identity of the French general, finally overcome her devotion to the tyrannic custom.

Humphreys' work on *The Widow of Malabar* did not keep him from enjoying life with the Washington family. Washington's diaries, for example, give a vivid picture of Humphreys dining with the family and their friends. Throughout November and December 1787, Humphreys hunted fox with Washington and Lear. He enjoyed the Christmas pies with the family, accompanied Washington on his visits around the plantations and elsewhere, and often attended Sunday services with the entire family. In all, Humphreys spent an idyllic life as part of the family of the man who seems by that time to have become a surrogate father to him. But his time was also spent in literary activity. Not only had he been writing *The Widow of Malabar,* but he was also honored by Mathew Carey in the March 1788 issue of the *American Museum,* which devoted it entire poetry section to his work. His most important literary activity, however, was the preparation of his *Life of Putnam,* which he completed in time for the annual Fourth of July meeting of the Connecticut Society of the Cincinnati in 1788.

Although it is not often remembered today, *An Essay on the Life of the Honourable Major-General Israel Putnam* proved to be Humphreys' most enduring work. It was a popular success in the eighteenth century and was included in the 1790 *Miscellaneous Works.* It was also widely read in the nineteenth century with at least seven separate editions, plus an unknown number of impressions and reprints, the last of which was published in New York in 1856. Its popularity is evidenced by James Fenimore Cooper, who was so familiar with it that he borrowed both the broad outline and specific details of frontier warfare for *The Last of the Mohicans.*[45]

No national history had yet been written in 1788, and those who sought details of the American past turned instead to local history and biography. Humphreys' *Life of Putnam* appears to have been the first popular biography of an American hero and as such may have served as model for the many others that followed. In it he joined personal memoir and piety to create a character quite different from the real Putnam. Humphreys' position in the history of American biography—its mythmaking stage—is pivotal, therefore, and worthy of more notice than it currently receives.

Humphreys prefaced his *Life of Putnam* with a letter to his old friend Jeremiah Wadsworth, then President of the Connecticut Society of the Cincinnati. He explained why he chose Putnam and once again stated the close relationship between "amusement and instruction" in literature: "An essay on the life of a person so elevated in military rank, and so conversant in extraordinary scenes, could not be destitute of amusement and instruction, and would possess the advantage of presenting for imitation a respectable model of public and private virtues." He went on to say he believed his to be "the first effort in Biography that has been made on this continent" and that it was therefore "laudable, whatever may be the failure in point of execution." Humphreys was apparently ignorant of Cotton Mather's *Magnalia,* or perhaps had discounted it as an example of the same kind of biographical writing he had done. He may well have sensed a distinction between his own work and Mather's, even though they shared a didactic and commemorative motive as well as a hagiographic leaning toward the encouragement of morality. For one thing, Humphreys' *Life of Putnam* had a broader, nationalistic appeal than Mather's ecclesiastical history. Moreover, Humphreys' biography was a single volume devoted entirely to its subject, while Mather's *Magnalia* was an exhaustive compilation of the spiritual lives of New England divines. Finally, unlike Mather, Humphreys constructed his *Life of Putnam* from a unique combination of memoir, episode, and anecdote. Whether or not the difference in intention and performance between his own work and Mather's warrants the statement that his was the first biography written in America, however, is debatable.

As biography, the book is curiously constructed in two parts, the first being largely romance and the second personal memoir. The two parts are roughly equivalent in length, although the latter half, Humphreys' memoirs of the war years, is actually a few pages longer than the former, which is a history of Putnam's entire life until the Revolution. The book ends with Putnam's stroke in December 1779. The first half is anecdotal and romantic, and is largely responsible for the book's mythmaking quality. This section shows Putnam descending with a gun and torch into the den of a ferocious "she-wolf" that had killed untold numbers of local sheep and goats. This section is notable, too, for showing the daring Putnam as an Indian fighter during the French and Indian War, particularly his numerous hairbreadth escapes. Throughout, it dramatizes Putnam's intelligence, bravery, and humanity, creating a larger-than-life portrait.

It seems that Humphreys' tone of uncritical admiration was a genuine expression of his feeling for the old warrior. It should be noted at the same time, however, that many of the details of this section had been transmitted to Humphreys by Dr. Albigence Waldo, whom Humphreys acknowledged early in the *Life*. Waldo had recorded many anecdotes "communicated to him by General Putnam." Humphreys, therefore, retold stories that had originally been dictated by Putnam and later written down by Waldo. Humphreys' treatment of this information was secondhand, but, since the material fit neatly into his hagiographic plan, he saw no need to confirm the anecdotes before making them a permanent part of the biography. That they were traceable to Putnam himself established their veracity beyond reasonable doubt—at least so far as Humphreys was concerned.

The *Life of Putnam* is less than reliable as a record of Putnam's life. Nonetheless, the book has historical and literary interest both as biography and as an early harbinger of American romances. From the very first advertisement for the *Life,* appearing in the *Connecticut Courant* (Hartford, 1 September 1788) and the *Connecticut Journal* (New Haven, 3 September 1788), the merging of biography and romance was recognized: "Many occurences in [Putnam's] earlier life almost surpass the bounds of credibility and equal the astonishing fictions of romance." Humphreys' contribution to Romantic fiction is, therefore, substantial, and an argument might well be made for Humphreys as one of America's earliest writers of romances. The second section of Humphreys' *Life of Putnam* is based largely on firsthand observation, and in this part the information is more trustworthy; but if the information is more accurate, the reading is slower. The romantic sections of the *Life of Putnam* gave the book its flavor and accounted for its great contemporary popularity.

Humphreys spent the last half of 1788 with the Washington family in much the same manner as the first. Important political news, however, gave these months extra interest for everyone. It became known late in the summer that eleven of thirteen states had ratified the Constitution and that elections for president and vice-president were to be held in January. While the family awaited the expected results, the day-to-day life at Mount Vernon changed very little.

During the fall and winter Humphreys continued his literary pursuits. In a rare direct statement about America's literary prospects, made in a letter to Thomas Jefferson, Humphreys wrote, "As much attention is paid to the cultivation of literature as can be expected in a country that is so young and whose inhabitants are obliged to apply themselves to some profession for a maintenance."[46] Perhaps the simple truth of the statement was borne home to Humphreys at this time because he realized that he was *not* applying himself to a profession for his maintenance. And, in fact, this freedom gave him considerable opportunity to engage in literary work. One of his more satisfying projects was the publication of a book of poems. Entitled simply *Poems,* the book was published by Mathew Carey in January 1789. It contains the most important work in verse that Humphreys had done to that time: the Fairfield elegy, the "Letter to a Young Lady in Boston," the "Address to the Armies," the elegy on de Hart, "The Monkey Who Shaved Himself," the "Ode to Laura," "A Song," "An Epithalamium," "Happiness of America," the epitaph for Scammel, "Mount-Vernon: An Ode," "Anacreontic," and "The Genius of America." The title page of the book stated that this was the "second edition:—with several additions." Apparently the seven poems that had appeared in the *American Museum* in 1788 were considered the first "edition"; the fragile, paperbound *Poems* was in reality, however, the first true collection of Humphreys' poetry.

Official news of Washington's election reached Mount Vernon by special messenger on 14 April 1789. There had been no doubt about the outcome, for Humphreys had written on 7 April to General Williams explaining the route Washington would be taking to New York.[47] On the sixteenth, Washington recorded in his diary: "About ten o'clock I bade adieu to Mount Vernon, to private life, and to domestic felicity, and, with a mind oppressed with more anxious and painful sensations than I have words to express, set out for New York in company with Mr. Thomson and Colonel Humphreys."[48]

Secretary and Secret Agent

Washington had four secretaries at the time of his inauguration, on 30 April. Lear was the senior secretary and Humphreys was next in rank. Because of his experience abroad and his penchant for dignified formality, Humphreys was put in charge of ceremonies and official protocol. His official responsibilities afforded him enough free time to write and deliver a short oration, "On the Political Situation of the United States of America," at the 1789 Independence Day celebration of the Connecticut Society of the Cincinnati. He spoke of the Revolution, the Articles of Confederation, and the new Constitution, and the prospects for future happiness. The essay synthesized many ideas that had appeared elsewhere in Humphreys' work, like his disapproval of the "licentious appetites" and the "corrupted morals" of men and the need for a strong central government. What is new in this address is his publicly stated approval of the Constitution.

After spending two and a half months as one of three commissioners sent by George Washington to explore treaty possibilities with the Creek Indians, Humphreys returned to New York in late November and resumed his customary secretarial role for Washington. The winter of 1789–90 was thus spent comfortably, performing the familiar duties for which he was well rehearsed. However, during late spring and early summer 1790, affairs between the United States and England, Spain, and Portugal had developed into the kind of delicate diplomatic problem which demanded a response from the President. That response was destined to mold the next twelve years for David Humphreys.

In the first place, relations between Spain and England were faltering and war between them was distinctly possible. By becoming Spain's ally, the United States, it was felt, would be in a much better position to negotiate rights to the Mississippi River. It was hoped, too, that Spain might even be able to dislodge the British from western posts, which were to have been turned over long before.

In addition, Portugal, which had enjoyed trade arrangements with several individual states, was the first country to petition the United States to establish diplomatic relations. Delicate questions pertaining to the level of exchanged diplomats therefore arose for the first time.[49] Washington decided to send a secret agent to Europe, one who was to "avoid all suspicion of being on any public business," and that agent was David Humphreys.[50] His tasks were to brief William Carmichael, United States chargé d'affaires in Madrid, about the administration's Mississippi River policy and to arrange the exchange of diplomatic missions with Lisbon.

Humphreys left for England on 1 September 1790, fully aware of the delicacy of his mission and eager to accept a new challenge. On the other hand, however, he was deeply sorry to be leaving his patron and friend. He wrote to Washington on the eve of his voyage that it had been difficult to say goodbye: "I found the burden on my heart choaked the passage of utterance."[51]

In one final literary effort before leaving for Europe, Humphreys completed another collection of his works. It was published in 1790 as *Miscellaneous Works* and included his important poems, his play, and his *Life of Putnam*. In addition to these, Humphreys published here for the only time his prologue and epilogue to Racine's *Athaliah*. The concluding lines of the prologue sounded a familiar note in Humphreys' work—a call for the young nation's poets to commemorate their national heroes:

> Haste, haste, ye sons of song, call glory forth,
> And dare display your great compatriots' worth;
> Thence future ages will not view unmov'd,
> What Adams, Jay, and WASHINGTON approv'd! (*MW*, 1790, 178)

Chapter Four

Diplomat

Humphreys' special assignment to London, Lisbon, and Madrid stretched into permanent appointments in the latter capitals. What had originally been planned as a one year occupation became the work of twelve, and the direction of Humphreys' life changed dramatically. Throughout the 1790s, he developed into the United States' most efficient and reliable ambassador on the Iberian peninsula. His role, modest at first, grew quickly as his diplomatic talents became increasingly apparent to Washington, who came to depend heavily on Humphreys' prolific correspondence. In 1793 Humphreys was commissioned to negotiate directly with the Dey of Algiers for the release of American prisoners, on whose behalf he had spoken poetically some eight years earlier in "Happiness of America." After many frustrating delays, the captives were released early in 1796. Although Humphreys put in motion all the machinery that led to their release, his responsibility for it is not widely recognized. Washington, however, did recognize the conscientious and competent work of his former aide by appointing him in June 1796, America's first minister plenipotentiary to the court at Madrid. He remained in that position until, in a flagrantly political action, he was recalled by Thomas Jefferson in the spring of 1801.

During his twelve years in Europe, Humphreys never actually abandoned poetry, although he seems to have written only sporadically. While he did produce seven sonnets, he apparently stopped composing the occasional verse he had written so often in the past. When he did write, he produced long addresses to citizens of the United States, verse orations which served as a formal restatement of his own patriotic faith. He wrote the first of these poems, "On Industry," in 1792; the second, "On the Love of Country" in 1799; and the third, the "Elegy" on Washington's death, in 1800. These dates correspond exactly to the difficulty of Humphreys' diplomatic chores: "Industry" appears to have been written before Humphreys began his tenure as minister resident in Lisbon. The years of negotiation, 1793–96, appear to have occupied Humphreys totally, leaving little time for poetry. When he arrived at Madrid in August 1797, however, Humphreys' diplomatic work was less urgent, allowing him time in 1798 to begin writing "Love of Country," delivered in Madrid on the Fourth of July in 1799. Similarly, the "Elegy" was delivered as a July Fourth oration the next year. Finding time was difficult, but for Humphreys, poetry and diplomacy were, indeed, compatible.

Inheriting a Commission

By October 1790 Humphreys had completed his transatlantic journey and was in London writing the first of more than 500 official and semiofficial letters completed during the next twelve years. Humphreys' diplomatic communications cover a wide range of subjects, frequently wandering to include personal details of friends and foes at court; they touch on every conceivable international topic, from the threat and reality of war to observations on the efficiency and reliability of the diplomats with whom he associated. By late October Humphreys had booked passage to Lisbon. He wrote with concern to Thomas Jefferson that his name had been mentioned frequently at the New York Coffee House, "with speculations on the cause of my coming here, at this time."[1] Commenting further on his effectiveness as secret agent, he wrote to Washington that despite his efforts to avoid "all appearances of curious enquiry or mysterious reserve . . . somebody has written to Paris, describing a person, once a Colonel, in the American Army, as now employed here in intrigues relative to the Spanish War."[2] That he was popular in his own right and known, too, as an intimate friend of President Washington had clearly marked him as an object of political speculation, and Humphreys was therefore anxious to be away from England to maintain whatever was left of his anonymity.

On 19 November Humphreys arrived at Lisbon and immediately began preparing for his trip to Madrid, to brief William Carmichael about the administration's Mississippi River policy. Before departing, however, Humphreys spoke to the Chevalier de Pinto, Portugal's minister of foreign affairs, about the planned exchange of diplomatic missions. Humphreys had a slight advantage because the chevalier, having known Humphreys from 1785–86, was well disposed toward him. On behalf of the President and Secretary of State, Humphreys pointed out that the diplomatic exchange of full ministers would prove too costly for the United States, which preferred the diplomats to be at the level of chargé d'affaires. The problem, however, proved more difficult to resolve than Washington or Jefferson had anticipated. Queen Maria had already appointed a minister resident from the court at Lisbon to the United States. Moreover, according to the chevalier, the Portuguese government was unable to find anyone of sufficient character who was willing to make such a long trip for a lesser rank.[3] Diplomatic courtesy would not allow the queen to receive a diplomat of inferior rank to the one she sent. Complicating the business still further, the man selected by the queen as minister resident to the United States, Chevalier de Freire, had already been recalled from his position in London and replaced by the former ambassador to Rome. In the face of all this Portuguese diplomatic activity, Humphreys could only reiterate that the United States as a young nation did not wish to incur the great expense of maintaining a minister resident at Lisbon.

In a report to Washington marked "(Secret)" and dated from Lisbon on 30 November, Humphreys explained the situation, commenting that a Portuguese reversal of policy was unlikely. Even worse, he believed American intransigence would actually threaten the exchange. He suggested that if, indeed, the question of cost was the only one standing in the way of an exchange of ministers, then he himself would accept the position of minister resident to the court at Lisbon with the annual salary of a chargé d'affaires. He reasoned that because he was unmarried, such a salary would allow him to "establish a Household and with good economy, live decently in such a manner as not to discredit myself, or my nation. . . ."[4] With that, Humphreys turned his attention to the overland trip of 500 miles to Madrid.

He arrived in the middle of December and found the diplomatic atmosphere less cordial to the American delegation than in Lisbon.

Carmichael held the rank of chargé d'affaires, a position that often kept him from getting a full hearing at the Spanish court. Moreover, the Spanish government was cool to the American legation over anticipated American land claims in the Louisiana territory. When Humphreys met Carmichael, he explained that it was a matter of the utmost importance for the United States to obtain rights to navigate the Mississippi and establish a port at its mouth. Jefferson's letter to Carmichael said that Humphreys, "possessing the sentiments of the Executive on this subject," had come to Madrid to explain the situation thoroughly. According to Jefferson, Americans living on or near the Mississippi might soon become impatient and belligerent; however, "neither themselves nor their rights will ever be abandoned by us."[5] His meaning was clear—as were Carmichael's responsibilities. Humphreys, however, was not optimistic: Carmichael's low rank, poor health, and bad attitude argued against any satisfactory negotiation of the "navigation-port" problem.

Meanwhile, back in the United States, Washington sent a special message to the Senate on 18 February in which he explained the situation in Portugal. After careful consideration, Washington nominated Humphreys as minister resident. By 15 March the Senate had confirmed the nomination and by 22 May Humphreys was presented to Queen Maria. His duties in 1791 did not include overseeing negotiations with the Barbary states for the release of American prisoners, though certainly this was on his mind. Humphreys' long-simmering anger with the pirates of the Barbary states over the capture of American seamen dated from 1785–86, to his original conclusion to "Happiness of America," which had included over 400 lines on the subject. He had tried in that poem to excite a militaristic patriotism and had recommended a rather muscular solution to the problem of the Barbary pirates: he urged Americans to rise up and smite the new enemies as they had their British oppressors earlier. The original "Happiness of America" contained the following climactic apostrophe to Algiers:

> Woe to proud Algiers; to your princes woe!
> Your pride is falling with your youths laid low—
> Woe to ye people, woe, distress, and fears!
> Your hour is come to drink the cup of tears:

A ghastly paleness gathers on your cheeks,
While mem'ry haunts your ears with captive shrieks;
Then stifled conscience wak'ning dares to cry,
"Think on your crimson crimes, despair and die."—
Then ruin comes, with fire, and sword, and blood,
And men shall ask, "Where once your cities stood?"[6]

Following these lines came a thirty-one-line stanza describing a vision of the absolute ruin of Algiers after war with the United States. Five years before his appointment as minister resident in Lisbon, then, Humphreys had vividly expressed his anger toward the Barbary states, and finally, in 1791, his influence in this area had begun to develop.

In 1791 Jefferson was still eager to free the Algerine captives, but his sense of urgency was considerably reduced. The official posture of the secretary of state was to appear indifferent so the demanded ransom might not be too great. A cash settlement had been arranged with Morocco, but not with Algiers, Tunis, or Tripoli. The principal threat came from the Dey of Algiers. The diplomatic community believed that a peace treaty with Algiers, including a cash settlement and annual tribute, would free the captives and buy protection for American shipping in the Mediterranean. Although this was international terrorism and blackmail, freeing the captives was still desirable; nonetheless, Thomas Jefferson gave the affair low priority in 1791.

On 1 June 1792 John Paul Jones was commissioned by Washington to negotiate with the Dey of Algiers. Jones was empowered to pay $40,000 for the release of the captives and $25,000 annually in tribute thereafter, for as long as the treaty was in effect. Jones's instructions were carried to London by Thomas Pinckney, who was then on his way there to assume duties as the American minister plenipotentiary. When Pinckney arrived, however, he learned that Jones had died in Paris on 18 July. Jefferson had prepared duplicate orders for Thomas Barclay in Morocco, which he sent with Pinckney to be used only in the event of Jones's death. Barclay was in Lisbon, awaiting the conclusion of the Moroccan war for the succession of the imperial throne so that he might then be able to resume efforts to have the Moroccan government ratify the treaty with the United

States. Pinckney's orders to Barclay were delayed for several months, but, soon after they were finally delivered, Barclay, too, died. Eight months had elapsed since Congress had commissioned John Paul Jones, but negotiations with the Dey had not yet begun.

On 8 February Humphreys wrote to George Washington suggesting that he be appointed to conclude the commission of John Paul Jones and Thomas Barclay. Washington and Jefferson, however, had already determined to give Humphreys the commission. News of the appointment was carried to Lisbon by Nathaniel Cutting, who was named secretary to Humphreys. Cutting was an expert accountant, a necessary skill that complemented nicely Humphreys' diplomatic skills. Humphreys was finally in charge of ransoming the Algerine captives; unfortunately, however, it took six months for him to learn of his commission because Cutting had been given several diplomatic errands and did not actually arrive in Lisbon until 28 August 1793.[7]

Poetry from Lisbon

On 20 June 1792, more than a full year before Nathaniel Cutting arrived at Lisbon with instructions for Humphreys to assume the aborted mission of John Paul Jones and Thomas Barclay, Humphreys wrote a personal letter to the widow of Nathaniel Greene. The letter is light, breezy, and slightly nostalgic. He said he would like to have written a "long kind of conversation letter," but "I frankly acknowledge that I am good for nothing at the pen." He reported that he was filling up his leisure hours by writing a poem, which, he said, resulted from finding Lisbon's "climate & situation, sufficiently agreeable."[8] He praised "the fragrant shades of Cintra's citron groves" and "rural monserat." In the final section he described Cintra's "gay fruitage mix'd with families of flow'rs." Yet, despite being smitten by Portugal's charms, Humphreys concluded on a more typically nationalistic note:

> Reclin'd ev'n there, beneath refreshing Skies,
> Still for my natal Land new longings rise:
> Remembrance goads this form, by seas confin'd,
> While all my Country rushes on my mind.

Rous'd at the name . . . I feel the patriot heat,
Burn in my bosom, in my pulses beat,
And wake unutterable thoughts. My lyre,
Though tortures for expression tear thy wire,
The still fond wish remains, as it began,
"Heav'n made that Land the blest retreat of Man."

This fragment indicates Humphreys' continuing passion for poetry in the summer of 1792; left to his own devices, and without more pressing business at hand, Humphreys invariably turned to poetry.

Shortly afterward, Humphreys mailed a more important example of his poetry to the United States. On 23 July 1792, he enclosed in a letter to George Washington the manuscript of his "Poem on the National Industry of the U.S.": "As far as I can judge of my own heart, I conceived myself to have been animated by love of Country in writing the Poem. I own I have received pleasure in composing, however others may or not in perusing it, for it is not for me to decide how I have succeeded in the execution. I have endeavoured to polish the versification as highly as in anything I have before written. . . . The sentiments, I know, are such as comport perfectly well with patriotism & good morals. . . ."[9] To Humphreys, no motivation could have been purer than that which "comport[ed] perfectly well with patriotism & good morals"— clearly one and the same thing.

The 1792 "Industry" contains an apostrophe to Industry in its exordium. The narration, with characteristically heavy dependence on apostrophe, rhetorical questions, and exclamations, is about American education, religion, medicine, and farming; it also contains some thirty-five compassionate lines on Negro slavery, fifty devotional lines on American womanhood, and twenty-five harsh lines on American Indians. After paying some minor attention to American sailors and soldiers, Humphreys wrote some fifty concluding lines in another call to arms against Algiers, similar in spirit to the original conclusion in "Happiness of America." By allowing the poem to drift rather aimlessly into a denunciation of Algiers, a subject that was obviously on Humphreys' mind in the early 1790s, he indulged himself but sacrificed his art, for the conclusion fit the poem poorly. In fact, the 1792 "Industry" enjoys a few inspired moments but lacks the thematic cohesiveness achieved in the 1804 version. The improvement of the latter version is due to the elimination of the Algerine section altogether and the inclusion of an important new section on Connecticut. In the 1804 "Industry" Humphreys would present the industriousness of the people of Connecticut as a mechanism for binding the fabric of a free society.

Within the fairly short 1792 "Industry" (463 lines compared to 672 in the 1804 version), Humphreys wrote such predictable lines as "BLOW YE TRUMPET!—sound—oh, sound th'alarms— / To arms—to arms—brave citizens! to arms—[.]" Yet at least one stanza rises above the predictable in its emphasis on the importance of industry to the human spirit. Poetically this is a short, self-contained lyric that builds nicely to its own climax:

> What, but rough effort, strengthens ev'ry part,
> Ennerves the arm, and fortifies the heart?
> What gives our Seamen steadiness of soul,
> When bursting thunders rend the red'ning pole,
> When down the black'ning clouds, in streams that bend
> Round the tall top-masts, livid fires descend;
> When howling winds, in wild gyrations fly,
> And night sits frantic on the scowling sky?

The frightful image of a storm at sea is capped with the vivid description of a "frantic" night superimposed on a "scowling sky." Like the whole poem, this stanza is an expression of the Puritan work ethic, here stripped of its religious underpinnings. The poem typifies late eighteenth-century American thinking in that the work ethic had been secularized but remained intact; its value had become nationalistic rather than spiritual.

Freeing the Algerine Captives

Humphreys and Cutting left Lisbon for Gibraltar on 17 September 1793, and from there they traveled to Valencia and Alicante, Spanish coastal towns on the Mediterranean. When notified, however, that David Humphreys was waiting for permission to enter Algiers under a special commission from America, the Dey of Algiers refused unequivocally to see him. The Dey's snub meant that once again

American efforts to free the Algerine captives had been thwarted, and that another eight months had elapsed with no progress having been made.

Frustrated and angry, Humphreys reported his treatment at the hands of the Dey in a letter of 23 November 1793 to George Washington. The letter reveals Humphreys' continued willingness to solve the problem militarily: "A naval force has now . . . become indispensable. . . . It will not, I am confident, escape your recollection that the *whole Nation* ought, from every sentiment of patriotism liberty & humanity, to be roused into exertion, *as one Man*." He also suggested a day of fasting and prayer to be declared "for the liberation of our fellow Citizens from Slavery."[10] Meanwhile, three more vessels had been captured, bringing the total number to thirteen. Humphreys and Cutting, though, had no alternative but to leave Alicante for Madrid, which they did on 12 December. By 21 January they had returned to Lisbon.

The year 1794 was another frustrating one. In January Jefferson finally made good his oft-repeated intention to resign as secretary of state; he was replaced by Edmund Randolph. During the transition period, negotiations seemed permanently stalled. In late November Humphreys was still hamstrung, partly because the Dey refused to see him and partly because he awaited a renewed authorization to negotiate. He continued to hope that a new authorization would allow him to offer the Dey a more tempting settlement. With matters having reached this year-long impasse, Humphreys took it upon himself to return home to discuss the complicated affair with Washington. Given a full year of what seemed official inattention to the plight of the captives, he considered that his return to the United States, while irregular, would be the fastest and most reliable way of getting necessary information and effecting the desired results.

Humphreys left Lisbon on 4 December and arrived at Newport on 3 February 1795. Passing him en route was a letter from Secretary of State Randolph which would have made the trip unnecessary. Randolph admitted in that letter that he had not kept Humphreys fully abreast of news regarding the Algerine captives, adding cryptically that he thought it "best to postpone particular remarks, until the conclusion of the business." Humphreys' new authorization included some $800,000, "to sooth the Dey into a peace."[11] Since Humphreys did not return to Lisbon until late November 1795, his trip to the United States, while predicated on the best of motives, was translated into a net loss of another full year in negotiations.

When they discussed the matter, Humphreys, Washington, and Randolph decided that Humphreys should try to enlist the aid of France, then at peace with Algiers. They also decided to try to get Humphreys' friend Joel Barlow, who was then in Paris with French and American citizenship, as agent to deal with the Dey. Any agreements that Barlow might reach were to be forwarded to Humphreys in Lisbon for final approval and signature before being sent to the United States. With this new plan of action, Humphreys sailed for Gibraltar on 8 April. He was accompanied by Joseph Donaldson of Philadelphia, who replaced Cutting as Humphreys' secretary. Donaldson was also named the Consul to Tunis and Tripoli; in this capacity he was to be an arm of Humphreys in preliminary investigations with Algiers into the possibility of a peace and the release of the captives. They arrived at Gibraltar on 24 May.

Donaldson and Humphreys separated at Gibraltar. Humphreys traveled directly to France, reaching Havre on 26 June. From there he traveled by horse to Paris and delivered official dispatches to James Monroe, then Minister to France. Humphreys arrived in Paris on about the first of July. Monroe's diplomatic mission was difficult during those days of the French Revolution, and he was not pleased with the directive which had him seek official French aid for America in its own troubled foreign relations with Algiers. Regardless, he did obtain France's aid and managed to have Barlow appointed special agent working on behalf of both countries. But shortly before Barlow was to leave for Algiers, the astonishing news was received that Donaldson, on his own, had actually concluded a treaty with the Dey.

Humphreys, however, had left Paris on 14 September, before news of Donaldson's peace treaty with the Dey had arrived. When he reached Havre on his way back to Lisbon, he found the captain of the *Sophia* ill; the ship did not sail until 5 October. Waiting to return to Lisbon, Humphreys turned his thoughts to the incredible complications which had attended his best efforts to free the Algerine captives, as yet ignorant of this last ironic complication. Disappointed and discouraged, he wrote a letter in which he counseled a young nephew to "chuse any profession, but a public life.—From which, I know by experience *(even though one be tolerably successful)* little is to be gained but care & trouble."[12] On 17 November, nearly a full year after he had left, Humphreys was back in Lisbon.

Donaldson's agreement with the Dey was satisfactory to Humphreys when he heard of it on 18 November. Its ratification, however, depended on the actual payment due, and final arrangements for payment had yet to be made. In January 1796, Barlow left Paris for Algiers in the capacity of Temporary Agent to the Dey. Both he and Donaldson, together or separately, were empowered to negotiate as necessary. The money, however, proved more difficult to get than they had anticipated, and they found it necessary in the end to offer the Dey an American frigate in order to bind the treaty. In the meantime, however, he finally agreed to free the captives.

In Madrid, too, resolution of long-standing problems was in sight. William Short had succeeded Carmichael as chief American diplomat in May 1794, but he, too, was unable to hammer out a satisfactory treaty with Spain. In the summer of 1795, Thomas Pinckney, minister plenipotentiary at London, was appointed special envoy to the court of Madrid. Pinckney succeeded in negotiating the Treaty of San Lorenzo (signed 27 October 1795 and ratified 3 March 1796), which gave the United States free navigation of the Mississippi and the right of deposit at New Orleans. After the successful negotiations had been completed, Pinckney and Short left Madrid, leaving the ministry to the Spanish court vacant.

Despite the circuitous route to peace that Humphreys had to travel, preliminary agreements with all four Barbary powers were finally effected under his authority, and he was appointed on 20 May 1796, America's first full minister plenipotentiary to the court at Madrid. Timothy Pickering, who succeeded Edmund Randolph as secretary of state, wrote to Humphreys on 11 June 1796 announcing the appointment. Humphreys was instructed, however, to complete the peace treaties with the Barbary states before moving to Madrid to assume his duties. It took about a year longer before the treaties were completed and Humphreys could leave Lisbon.[13]

Humphreys knew that he had done everything possible for the Algerine captives, yet for all his strong feelings and active participation, little actual progress seemed traceable to him. His six-month effort to see the Dey had met with frustrating obdurateness; all of 1794 was frittered away as he waited impatiently for instructions and authorization to offer the Dey a significant cash settlement; his trip to America produced a plan but lost another year; and, finally, the months between November 1795 and February 1796 produced more frustration as he tried to effect the transfer of necessary funds from one European capital to another. He might have taken some consolation by reflecting that the very presence of Donaldson and Barlow in Algiers was a direct result of his trip to the United States and that, while he was denied the satisfaction of being at the peace talks, he was truly the force which set in motion a final agreement.

The year between June 1796 and June 1797 saw the last correspondence between Washington and Humphreys. Washington wrote on 1 June, reflecting his weariness at being criticized regularly in the gazettes, yet maintaining as well his belief in the rightness of his decisions and policies. Looking toward retirement, he invited Humphreys to join him: "Whenever you shall think with the Poet or Philosopher 'that the Post of honor is a private Station' and may be disposed to enjoy yourself in my Shades—I do not mean the Shades below—where, if you put it of[f] long[,] I may be reclining, I can only repeat that you will meet with the same cordial reception at Mount Vernon, that you have always found at that place."[14] Humphreys' sense of public duty, which included his recent appointment as minister plenipotentiary at Madrid, kept him from accepting the offer. But there was another reason, too, for Humphreys was about to marry Miss Ann Frances Bulkeley, whose family Humphreys had known professionally as wealthy bankers and personally as friends since at least 1791 in Lisbon. Humphreys was nearly forty-five when he wrote to Washington of his forthcoming marriage: "If I shall not be as completely happy as my nature will allow, I know it will not be for want of disposition in the Lady in question to make me so. And I am conscious She has it more in her

power than any other person with whom I have been acquainted."[15]
For the first time since he had become Washington's aide in June
1780, Humphreys found it impossible to put himself at the disposal
of the one person he valued highest among men.

Humphreys remained in Madrid for three and a half years as
minister plenipotentiary. With the thorny business of the Barbary
pirates satisfactorily behind him, and the delicate negotiations regarding the Mississippi having been settled by Thomas Pinckney,
Humphreys passed his tenure in Madrid without the severe diplomatic tensions that had prevailed between 1791 and 1796.

Poetry from Madrid

Humphreys completed two long poems in Madrid, both delivered
as July Fourth orations for Americans in the Spanish capital: "A
Poem on the Love of Country" (1799) and "A Poem of the Death
of General Washington" (1800). Both were published for the first
time in *Miscellaneous Works* (1804), where, in the "Original Preface,"
Humphreys maintained that "Love of Country" was a "dissertation
on, and the other an exemplification of, real Patriotism."[16] He
further described the poems in a letter to Jeremiah Olney in Providence: "Love of Country," he said, "contains (at least so far as I
have been able to express sentiments by words) a transcript of my
principles, and that on the Death of *General Washington, of my
feelings.*"[17]

In his dedication and advertisement to "Love of Country" Humphreys expressed anew his conviction that poetry and patriotism
were kindred. "To make use of poetry for strengthening patriotism,
promoting virtue, and extending happiness," he wrote, "is to bring
it back to its primitive exalted employments. The author . . . will
not suppress his predilection for consecrating to such pursuits whatever poetical talents he may possess" (*MW,* 124). The message here
is the same one that recurs throughout Humphreys' work, although
rarely did he express it so directly. Furthermore, he stated in the
advertisement his eighteenth-century sense that public service is
more important than personal gain or the gentlemanly avocation of
poetry. He took "a becoming pride in asserting, that, in indulging
his taste for poetry, he . . . never suspended his attention to the

public service. . . ." He maintained "that there can be no happiness without virtue, no liberty without morality, and no good public character without being at the same time a good private character" (*MW*, 125). Possibly observations like these were unnecessary and morally self-indulgent, but Humphreys quite clearly made them from a sincere belief that poetry and advancement must be made subordinate to serving the commonweal. To his credit, the philosophy stated here is a mirror image of his public record.

Also in the "Original Preface," Humphreys wrote a short statement of his literary principles. He rationalized first that if there should be "defects or imperfections of style" in either of his Madrid poems, they could be attributed to his long absence from the company of English-speaking people. He stressed that he had tried to keep in touch with the language of English poetry, particularly "the sweetness of [Pope's] versification," and that through attention to such *"delicacies,"* he hoped to arrive at true *"taste."* Then, in a single paragraph, unlike any other he had ever written, Humphreys addressed himself to poetic theory:

Whether a poet composes from enthusiasm or with meditation, the art of animating and keeping alive the curiosity of his readers is certainly least of all to be neglected. Nothing can compensate for the want, for without it his works will not be read. To create an interest, is to command attention. To make descriptions or reflections not merely entertaining, but even intelligible, perspicuity is indispensably requisite. . . . In attempting to make the clearness of his style in a degree the mirror of his mind, he [Humphreys himself] was solicitous to shun turgid diction, brilliant antithesis, unnatural conceits, affected figures, forced epithets, and, in general, all factitious ornament. Nor was he less anxious to avoid mistaking and admitting vulgarity for simplicity. . . . Pleased with the charms of novelty, and delighted with whatever is elevated, beautiful, elegant, lovely, and excellent in the *works* of the ancients and moderns, he should be happy to be found, in *his own,* to have aimed at originality without rashness, and imitation without servility. (*MW*, 122–23)

The key to understanding the spirit of Humphreys' poetry is his concentrated attention to what he called animation, "keeping alive the curiosity" of the reader. To achieve such animation, the poet must strive for perspicuity, which, in turn, is achieved through "luminous comprehension," "lucid order," "spirit and intelli-gence"—all aspects of clear thinking. As to writing a clear style (the "mirror of the mind"), the poet must avoid all artificialities of diction and figures. But, regardless of what he said about the de-sirability of simplicity in poetry, Humphreys by his own practice seemed unconvinced.

In "Love of Country" Humphreys wrote a verse oration containing fifty-three irregular verse paragraphs, 842 lines in all. In the three-stanza exordium he apostrophized his subject: "Hail *sacred Love of Country!* mystic tie! / That binds us to our native soil and sky!" (*MW,* 5–7). A patriotic spirit, he said, "indissolubly" bound his American audience to one another. With a rhetorical flourish he asked, "Will ye in love of country be surpast?" and then called on them: "Columbians! show ye love your favour'd lot, / By strong attachment to your natal spot" (*MW,* 31–32). The exordium is a challenge, picked up and answered in the long narration.

In the narration Humphreys began with a description of Creation and ended with American patriotic fervor—as though the one had been divinely meant to culminate in the other. In this inevitable progression, man is termed the "inheritor of earth's stupendous fabric," and—in true eighteenth-century fashion—Humphreys claimed it natural and right to love man after God and art after nature. Furthermore, those who love God, man, and nature will never be seduced by conquest, pride, and ambition, as had been the case with Ancient Rome, a state with a fatal national arrogance: "Perish the Roman pride a world that braves, / To make for one free state all nations slaves" (*MW,* 205–206). Did Rome not know that it, too, would one day sink into "black oblivion's gulf"?

After blasting Rome, Humphreys moved to kings, recognizing that while there have been some "righteous monarchs," most have been otherwise. But Humphreys also took aim at demagoguery, which he denounced with even greater spleen:

> While demagogues, to gain a boundless sway,
> The people flatter first, and next betray;
> With false professions real slavery bring,
> The guileful regents of the people-king! (*MW,* 267–70)

He called on patriots

> To save th'endanger'd state—unveil their guile!
> Man's rights and obligations reconcile!
> The demon-fury of the mob restrain,
> And bind licentiousness in law's strong chain!
>
> Though dire the desolation conqu'rors cause,
> When death behind them opes insatiate jaws;
> Though great the plagues, though horrible the curse
> Of despotism! still anarchy is worse—
> Undup'd by popular names, shall we not shun
> The *tyranny* of MANY as of ONE? (*MW*, 273–82)

The poem then describes false patriotism—first as it was corrupted into Roman conquest and the enslavement of other peoples, and second as it was currently being twisted in America into demagoguery and democracy. Clearly Humphreys' love of country was a Federalist's, one which put little or no faith in an unguided, democratic government. The poem proceeded from Creation to American Federalism according to a logical, if unlikely, progression.

The remainder of the narration defines genuine patriotism. For this Humphreys resorted to his familiar review of dead war heroes—Warren, Montgomery, Mercer, Laurens, Scammel, de Hart, and others. He called on American patriots to "promote the public weal." This, he said, should be achieved by avoiding the divisiveness of factions—familiar eighteenth-century advice, destined always to go unheeded. The narration culminates in another catalogue of American "patriot-chiefs": Washington, Gates, Greene, Putnam, Stirling, Sullivan, Lincoln, Knox, Morgan, Wayne, and others: "These chiefs illustrious led, in part, the host; / But who can name Columbia's countless boast?" (*MW*, 738–84). The four-stanza peroration contains Humphreys' memories of the Revolution some twenty-five years after the fact. He and his friends in Madrid longed sentimentally for home: "And oft in recollections sad, but dear, / I soothe long absence with a secret tear—" (*MW*, 795–96). He recalled his own youth in Connecticut, responding with passion and rhetoric to the very name of his country:

> I feel the patriotic heat
> Throb in my bosom, in my pulses beat,
> And on my visage glow. Though what I feel
> No words can tell—unutterable zeal!—(*MW*, 831–34)

If this poem is measured solely by the force of its patriotic spirit, one may reasonably call it successful. Its roundabout method focuses finally on a denunciation of demagoguery as false patriotism and a long, familiar, and belabored demonstration of true patriotism—all done within an oratorical framework and guided by Federalist principles.

The second poem, the "Elegy on Washington," was actually begun in 1796, long before Washington's death. Humphreys had written Washington on 1 January 1797: "If I should survive you, I shall . . . complete a poetical work . . . with the intention & belief of doing more justice to your character, than many an abler writer (less actuated by feeling) would be able to do. The few detached parts which I have executed, I own please me more than anything else which I have written."[18] Washington died on 14 December 1799, and on 22 February 1800, Humphreys wrote to Mrs. Washington: "Since the fatal news reached me, I have found my heart so much oppressed as not to be able to give vent to those effusions which can alone afford me some relief. . . . When my own grief shall become a little moderated, I propose to indulge my melancholy meditations in endeavouring to delineate such features of the character of the deceased father of his country, and such events of his interesting life, as have left the most indelible impressions on my mind."[19] Some five months later, in time for his Fourth of July oration in 1800, Humphreys delivered the "Elegy" in Madrid, dedicating it to Mrs. Washington.

The advertisement contains yet another statement of Humphreys' faith in patriotic poetry: "Is there nothing dreadfully sublime in the thunder of cannon, the charge of cavalry, and the moving line of infantry . . . ?" And what more than poetry is "more likely to elevate the rising generation to emulate the exalted deeds of their fathers . . . ?" In fact, Humphreys never had a theme better suited to his idea of what poetry should be than Washington's death. Here was a subject in which his great admiration for Washington as a man could mix with his faith in patriotic poetry. Moreover, Humphreys focused on Washington's life during the Revolution, creating the occasion once again to recall familiar scenes of heroic action. And, with Washington dead, Humphreys could be as effusive as he wanted without embarrassing Washington or being accused of having an ulterior motive for himself. As may be imagined, this particular "Elegy"—since it was a natural vehicle for Humphreys—contains all of his favorite poetic techniques: martial imagery, sincere devotion, and heightened rhetoric.

The twenty-line exordium contains two apostrophes (to Independence and Columbians), and is punctuated by no fewer than fifteen questions or exclamations. The early part of the narration describes the poet's "deep, immeasurable woe" over the death of Washington and contains a Gothic apostrophe to melancholy, in the Graveyard tradition, as well as a long apostrophe to the "orphan'd world" and the "poignant grief" that afflicted all—particularly the veterans of the Revolution. The main part of the narration—thirty-four of fifty-eight stanzas—is devoted to a biographical sketch of Washington, the man who provided by his integrity, virtue, and judgment an ideal "model for our youth." Humphreys moved through Washington's early military service with Braddock in the French and Indian War, and through his "happier days" (1763–75) as a judge, legislator, farmer, and husband. The Revolution, of course, is treated at great length—seventeen stanzas—with the greatest part of that devoted to a full-scale description of the Battle of Monmouth.

Because it is in verse, Humphreys' account of the Battle of Monmouth is both unique and interesting. The occasion provided Humphreys another opportunity to express his sense of the sublime, emphasizing the inspirational value of the "battle-sound":

> No blythesome lark that chaunts the birth of light,
> Nor soothing Philomela's notes at night,
> Nor virgin-voice responsive to her lyre,
> Can like the battle-sound the soul inspire. (*MW*, 397–400)

And amid the battle scene, Washington stood, like Achilles, leading
his forces into combat:

> Columbia, rallying round the godlike form,
> Swept o'er the dry sand like a mountain storm;
> The chief of chiefs, our foremost band before,
> Bade the dry sand be drunk with hostile gore. (MW, 437–40)

In no other Humphreys poem is there as vivid a battle scene as the
following, one of several in the poem:

> Then wrapp'd in dust and smoke the fight began,
> Steed furious springs on steed, and man on man:
> As fire-balls burst with startling flash at night,
> So clash Columbian sabres sparkling bright;
> Mixing with British blades, whose dancing flare
> Makes horrid circles, hissing high in air.
> From steely helms incessant lightnings flash,
> And death sits frequent in the ghastly gash.
> With inextinguishable rage, so rush'd
> Both hostile lines, by mutual fury push'd:
> So toil'd in blood, till drained of wonted force,
> Promiscuous fell the rider and the horse. (MW, 303–14)

After his seventeen-stanza review of Washington's role in the
Revolution, Humphreys completed the sketch of Washington's career. There are stanzas on Washington's fear of the threat of factions,
on his role as President of the Constitutional Convention, on his
election as President of the United States, and on his humanitarianism. There are stanzas on Indians and slavery, "that foul stain of
manhood." The sketch is completed with two short stanzas, one on
Washington's retirement to Mount Vernon and one on his death.
The peroration consists of three stanzas, building to an emotional
and rhetorical climax. On behalf of the country, Humphreys called
on all the dead "heroic chiefs" of the Revolution to "protect our
orphan'd land." He prayed God to "preserve, as thou hast made,
our nation free!" The poem concludes with a mystical vision of
Washington, whose final words to his country are an admonition
to worship God and love one's fellow man.

The "Elegy" for Washington is framed at beginning and end with deeply personal passages. The opening grieves his own loss as well as the country's, while the ending consoles Mrs. Washington. By far the greatest number of stanzas in the poem, however, are public. The poem is a laudatory oration, tracing the highlights of Washington's illustrious career. John Ward had said of such orations that they should be "set off and adorned with florid language and fine images, proper to grace the subject, which is naturally so well fitted to afford pleasure and entertainment."[20] For a poet like Humphreys, whose ideas of the sublime style and noble subjects met on the battlefield, no conceivable topic was more likely to produce a better poem than an elegy for George Washington.

The only other poems Humphreys produced while in Lisbon and Madrid were the sonnets, published together in chronological order in *Miscellaneous Works* (1804).[21] This was the first and only publication of Humphreys' twelve sonnets during his lifetime. The first four deal with topics related to the Revolution. Number V, "On Life," conveys the message, in the language of the poem, that "true life begins at death." Sonnets VI and VII are companion pieces written in 1795 on board the *Sophia,* which was then carrying Humphreys back to Europe after he had made his unauthorized return to the United States. Number VI, "On a Night-Storm at Sea," was a prayer to "speed the halcyon dawn and still the stormy wave." Number VII, "On a calm Morning which succeeded a Night-Storm at Sea," includes the "rapture of the hymning lay" as a prayerful thanks for deliverance. Number VIII, "On the Immortality of the Soul," contains much the same message as No. V, "On Life," that is, that the soul will not return to dust but be "Heav'n born" instead. Number IX, "On the Death of Major John Pallsgrave Wyllys," is an elegy for a friend from the Revolution who died in October 1790, in action with the Indians in the Ohio territory. Sonnet X, "On the Murders committed by the Jacobin Faction in the early Period of the French Revolution," stresses that the "blood-stain'd Jacobins," whom Humphreys characterized as "Murd'rers of millions under freedom's name!" will never quench "reason's flame" in Columbia. Sonnet XI, "Addressed to his Royal Highness the Prince of Brazil, on my taking leave of the Court of Lisbon, July,

1797," is a tribute to Portugal's "flow'ry fields" and "lost retreats."
Last is Sonnet XII, "On Receiving the News of the Death of General
Washington," which is a poetic tribute to Washington, written
before the more elaborate "Elegy" that followed.

All but the last sonnet are constructed in the same unique fashion
as the first five; two quintains follow an opening quatrain. The
rhymes in most of the poems link the first and second stanzas, while
the third introduces new rhymes. The last two lines of each sonnet
are a couplet. The sonnet on Washington, however, is a surprising
variation on this form:

> Hark! friends! what sobs of sorrows, moans of grief,
> On every gale, through every region spread!
> Hark! How the western world bewails our chief,
> Great Washington, his country's father dead!
>
> Our living light expiring with his breath,
> His bright example still illumes our way
> Through the dark valley of thy shadow, death!
> To realms on high of life without decay,
>
> Faint, he relied on heav'nly help alone,
> While conscience cheer'd th'inevitable hour;
> When fades the glare of grandeur, pomp of pow'r,
> And all the pageantry that gems a throne:
> Then from his hallow'd track, who shall entice
> Columbia's sons to tread the path of vice?

The format here in rhyme and stanzaic structure is Shakespearean,
though there is a slight modification in rhyme in lines nine through
twelve. The colon at the end of line twelve indicates that the final
two lines might well have been set off; in fact, they are isolated
both by rhyme and syntax. The poem, then, divides neatly into
three quatrains and a concluding couplet. While this sonnet is
minor, even in the Humphreys' canon, it is interesting structurally,
showing a sudden and unexplained turn from his experiments with
the Spenserian sonnet to the Shakespearean.[22]

The twelve sonnets published in *Miscellaneous Works* (1804) were
written at various times from 1776 to about 1799 and are not, for

the most part, related. Certainly, they are among the first to be published by an American—although the poems were probably revised before publication, making it impossible to know now what the originals may have been like. As published in 1804, however, the sonnets are serious and personal, marked by a uniformly somber tone. Because they were written at "remarkable periods and events" of Humphreys' life, the sonnets might be expected to offer particularly intimate pictures of their author. This, in fact, occurs but twice. Rarely elsewhere, however, did Humphreys reveal such a soul-searching concern for life after death as in numbers V, "On Life," and VIII, "On the Immortality of the Soul." Since neither poem has a definite biographical analogue—the death of his parents is a possibility—and since Humphreys never wrote any other poem quite like them, these two remain mysterious and intriguing, particularly for the inwardness of the subject matter. Humphreys is everywhere else a public poet, which is why these two private poems are set apart so dramatically. These two exceptions aside, however, nothing new or surprising is revealed about Humphreys in the sonnets.

Recall

With Thomas Jefferson's inauguration on 4 March 1801, Humphreys became aware of the full force of American political divisiveness as well as the insecurity of his own position. The professions of friendship that had passed between them in previous years were about to dissolve in the light of new political realities. Humphreys wrote a letter to the new president on 8 May, asking to be reappointed to his diplomatic post and to be remembered for past services. Summing up his position, he said, "In attention, industry, zeal & perseverance I know I have not been wanting."[23] He supported this claim with an impressively detailed statement of his accomplishments while in Madrid. Apparently Thomas Jefferson did not see Humphreys' service the same way: he had already written a letter of recall in mid-April. Jefferson's letter to Humphreys has not survived, nor has any letter which records Humphreys' feelings at the time he received the news. The tone of Humphreys' 8 May letter, however, reveals an acute anxiety for the security of his position.

Moreover, for a man like Humphreys, who saw himself as a dedicated and altruistic public servant, a rebuff from Jefferson, under any circumstances, could be construed only as a personal affront.

It was impossible for Humphreys to conclude his affairs very quickly after having spent nearly eleven years in European capitals. On 6 November 1801, he wrote to Timothy Dwight, asking him to look at available farms, settling on one "that is pleasantly situated & really capable of producing sufficient to support a family." He concluded, "I form the project of leaving Europe as soon after the rigour of winter shall be passed as I can make it convenient."[24]

Humphreys was returning to America, his public career concluded, but he was not returning without honor. The snub he had suffered from Jefferson could not, under the circumstances, humiliate him. For the remainder of his life he would be embittered toward the Republicans, but he did not allow his emotional response to interfere with the private enterprise he was already planning.[25] He saw himself as retiring from public life in much the same manner that Washington had longed to retire to Mount Vernon. In a way that he could not have fully realized, Humphreys was about to transfer the foundation of his social position from Europe's diplomatic soil to Connecticut's agricultural soil. He was about to become one of America's first captains of industry, a position destined to bring with it an acknowledged social position of its own.

Chapter Five
Gentleman Industrialist

Despite having spent twelve years as an effective and sophisticated ambassador in European capitals and having married a woman who moved easily in those circles, David Humphreys was not tempted to remain abroad. The uncertainty of his immediate future, however, was underscored by his foreign wife and his lack of a home or business in America. Moreover, the United States had changed, and Humphreys did not know what to expect, politically or otherwise. It was a time of anxieties and uncertainties: he had left for London in 1790, at age thirty-eight, a trusted advisor on special assignment for George Washington; he was returning in 1802, at age fifty, with his government career prematurely ended. Fortunately, Humphreys had sufficient courage and self-confidence to face an unsettled future.

Two important projects occupied Humphreys' attention as he prepared for his return home. First was the publication of his revised *Miscellaneous Works,* and second was the care and propagation of his prized flock of merino sheep, which he hoped would become the nucleus of a great woolen industry in America. Humphreys' success in these projects and his resolution at the same time of difficult personal problems as well as normal, day-to-day uncertainties are testimony to his strength of mind and purposefulness. Moreover, his accomplishments after 1802, achieved in the private sector without any government aid or encouragement, are, indeed, impressive—perhaps more so than anything he had done earlier.

Miscellaneous Works (1804)

As early as April 1800, Humphreys was writing to old friends in Europe and America announcing a projected new edition of his

Miscellaneous Works and seeking subscribers. He felt confident about the prospects, as his comment to John Trumbull (the painter) indicated: "From the interesting nature of the subject & from the partiality with which my Countrymen have judged my former compositions, in all probability the work will be sufficiently popular in America to occasion the circulation of a considerable number of copies."[1] And in November 1801, he wrote to Timothy Dwight that he intended to oversee personally the publication of his "Miscellanies," even supposing the "want of taste & the rage of party should not render the period peculiarly favorable for the purpose."[2]

Despite his doubts regarding the "want of taste" in America, Humphreys continued to be deeply involved with the production of his *Miscellaneous Works,* which appeared in April 1804, dedicated to the Duke de Rochfoucalt. The impressive subscription list of some five hundred names included the King and Queen of Spain; two presidents, Adams and Jefferson; and other famous names: Naphtali Dagget, Timothy Dwight, Aaron Dexter, Harrison G. Otis, Charles Pinckney, Susanna Rowson, William Short, Governor Caleb Strong (Massachusetts), Governor Jonathan Trumbull (Connecticut), and Noah Webster—among many another. The trail of names spread across Europe from London to Paris to Lisbon to Madrid to Gibraltar to Naples and, of course, through most of the states in America. The book itself was Humphreys' last extensive literary endeavor and included many revisions of earlier works as well as some that had never before been published—poetic, political, military, and scientific.

The first "new" poem in *Miscellaneous Works* was not new at all: "A Poem on the Future Glory of America." Of this 582-line poem, some 400 lines had been published earlier as the original conclusion to "Happiness of America," which appeared itself for the first time in 1804 in its abridged form. In all, "Future Glory" contains about 165 new lines, which comprise a special view of American commerce, laws, and internal improvements—including the new capital. Humphreys emphasized in these lines the sensibleness of avoiding wars and identified religion as the binding agent to end discord among the countries of the world. The other 400 lines, however, those borrowed from "Happiness of America," are very

warlike—a call to arms against the Barbary Pirates. The two movements of "Future Glory," then, are patched together, not having
grown organically from the same poetic impulse. This poem is
therefore one of Humphreys' strangest creations, lacking not only
organic unity but also thematic consistency. The harshness of his
attack on the Barbary states had been appropriate in the mid-1780s,
when he was writing "Happiness of America," but, after he had
played such an important role in the freeing of the Algerine captives
in the 1790s, Humphreys no doubt felt the warlike sentiments were
no longer necessary—either for the poem or for America's happiness.
He deleted the bellicose conclusion to the earlier poem; but rather
than give up the lines altogether, he incorporated them into a "new"
poem, softening the old message and tone by combining them with
a mellower, more peaceful strain. In fact, the two movements of
the narration of "Future Glory" do have some power; it is only when
they are viewed together, as companion elements of the same poem,
that they appear incompatible.

Despite the incongruous nature of its two-part narration, "Future
Glory" is otherwise fairly predictable. It begins with a twenty-line
exordium, which apostrophizes the poet's soul. The warlike part of
the narration begins with over 400 lines from the original "Happiness of America." Humphreys cited the problem created by the
Barbary states and evoked compassion for the Algerine captives.
Through a series of rhetorical questions, he asked how long Americans were to tolerate the enslavement of their people. The question
and answer represent Humphreys in his most characteristic pose,
the angry poet-turned-warrior:

> How long, Columbians dear! will ye complain
> Of wrongs unpunish'd on the midland main?
> In timid sloth shall injur'd brav'ry sleep?
> Awake! awake! avengers of the deep!
> Revenge! revenge! the voice of nature cries;
> Awake to glory, and to vengeance rise!
> To arms! to arms! ye bold, indignant bands!
> 'Tis Heav'n inspires, 'tis God himself commands:
> Save human nature from such deadly harms,
> By force of reason, or by force of arms. (*MW*, 121–30)

The assurance, bellicosity, and self-assertiveness of this part of "Future Glory" appear more likely to have been designed to bolster native self-confidence than to act in any real sense as a threat to the Barbary states.

The remainder of "Future Glory" is new—except for the final twenty-seven lines, also taken from "Happiness of America." This movement of the narration is directed to internal developments in the United States and reflects, in essence, Humphreys' revived interest in domestic concerns in 1801–1802. The poet feared anarchy and called for "Agrarian laws." He spoke of internal improvements, described the city of Washington, and wrote of America as a melting pot:

> To our new empire, lo! what crowds repair,
> Walk in its light and in its blessings share;
> For there th'oppress'd a place of refuge find,
> The last asylum for distrest mankind. (*MW*, 491–94)

The new stanzas conclude with a reminder that war destroys friends as well as foes, a surprisingly peaceful sentiment in an otherwise jingoistic poem. To this Humphreys added that the people of the United States were "God's chosen" and that religion was the power that would end discord and "join all nations in the leagues of Peace." The poem ends with a vision of happier days.

If Humphreys deleted the long call to arms from the conclusion to "Happiness of America" because it was no longer as appropriate in 1801 as it had been in 1786, one must question the judgment prompting him to relocate the lines into a "new" poem. It should have been clear to him that 400 lines could not effectively be taken out of a poem that had enjoyed such a great popular success as "Happiness of America." Conversely, "Future Glory" was not given enough new life to make it on its own. One is left with the uneasy feeling that the poem was hastily put together for *Miscellaneous Works* and that it was, overall, a mistake.

Humphreys so completely revised "A Poem on the Industry of the United States of America" for *Miscellaneous Works* that it should be considered a new work. The new subject of the 1804 "Industry" is Connecticut, which Humphreys hailed as the "model of free states," and praised for its bounty and opportunity, for its joys of rural toil and sober habits as well as its religious blessings and intellectual achievements. Interestingly, though, Humphreys did not begin to speak of Connecticut until line 400; the first 399 lines, paralleling the 1792 version, are about the blessedness of American toil in general. As in the 1792 version, there are sizable sections devoted to American farmers and women, the same strong denunciation of Negro slavery, and a harsh appraisal of the American Indian. The poem wanders, emphasizing throughout the importance of industry as the key ingredient in the development of healthy international, national, and local communities. He departed from the 1792 version by introducing Connecticut as the "model of free states": if the country could learn from Connecticut, and if the world could learn from the United States, industry would be viewed by all as the firmest foundation of social stability.

The section of "Industry" on Connecticut maintains simply that hard work elevates the human spirit. Toil is virtue and Connecticut is the home of the most virtuous. Humphreys delighted in God's blessing of Connecticut's education, medicine, justice, and intellectual achievement. He pictured Connecticut as the ideal microcosm: Connecticut's virtues should be the country's virtues. And in its final emphasis on property, the poem is distinctly Federalist:

> Ye junior patriots, listen! learn, my friends!
> How much your lot on industry depends:
> For God, a God of order, ne'er design'd
> Equal conditions for the human kind.
> Equality of rights your bliss maintains,
> While law protects what honest labour gains. (*MW*, 657–62)

The 1804 "Industry" demonstrated that David Humphreys' domestic politics changed not at all during the twelve years he had devoted, almost exclusively, to America's foreign policy.

The remaining new material published in *Miscellaneous Works* (1804) were prose statements called variously "thoughts," "remarks," "considerations," and the like.[3] In addition, five letters from George Washington were published, all written during Humphreys' period abroad and dated between 16 March 1791 and 26

June 1797. Arbitrarily deleted from *Miscellaneous Works* (1790) were the verse prologue and epilogue to Racine's *Athaliah* and the entire *Widow of Malabar.*

Each of the new prose pieces in *Miscellaneous Works* (1804) is predictable. Humphreys' "Remarks on the War between the United States and Tripoli" supported the policy he had long sought, that of protecting American commerce by a "national marine." "If any of my writings," he wrote, "have tended to promote its adoption, I shall receive a complete compensation for all the tedious correspondence, dangerous voyages, and troublesome negociations, in which I was for many years engaged."[4] His "Thoughts" on maintaining a navy has much the same message: "Protection [of American commerce] is our avowed object." In his "Consideration" on public defense, Humphreys showed his preference for a well-trained, organized militia to a standing army. Armies, he felt, could be misled by unscrupulous people: "God forbid we should ever be so infatuated as to swell the black catalogue of crimes, and augment the hereditary ills of our race, by the wanton effusion of human blood from motives of ambition, conquest, and aggrandisement." These passages reflect, as so many others do, Humphreys' belief in military readiness, although the last one seems to recognize an important distinction between true patriotism and one based on unbridled self-interest.

Few other collections by eighteenth-century Americans are as truly miscellaneous as Humphreys'. The long verse orations rightfully occupy center stage in the *Works* because these are his most complex literary creations. The occasional poems, however, show the breadth of Humphreys' literary interests, ranging as they do from elegies to sonnets with a wide variety of forms in between. The prose works, too, reflect a man with extraordinarily wide interests. In one work alone, the *Life of Putnam,* Humphreys wrote a book with value as history, biography, and romance. *Miscellaneous Works* is appropriately titled: it is the literary production of a public man, whose mind wandered with lively curiosity over a broad spectrum of topics.

Humphreysville

Humphreys and his wife arrived from Europe in the spring of 1802. By fall they had settled into a house on Beacon Hill in Boston, where they lived for the next four years. One supposes that Boston was chosen as a consideration for Mrs. Humphreys, who might well have found it disagreeable in rural Connecticut after living most of her life in European capitals. But despite the location of their home, Humphreys' life from 1802 until his death in 1818 was almost exclusively associated with Connecticut. Not only was he to become the most successful manufacturer of fine woolens in the United States—and that from his Connecticut mills—but he was also founder of the Connecticut Agricultural Society, a member of the Connecticut legislature, and a general in the Connecticut militia during the War of 1812. In addition, his use of child labor in the woolen factory at Rimmon Falls—renamed Humphreysville in 1808—was widely celebrated for its humanitarianism. Moreover, his scientific work on the breeding of sheep in Connecticut earned him election to the Royal Society in 1807. Finally, he produced his only original drama at Humphreysville, with players chosen from among the mill workers. Connecticut formed the center of Humphreys' interests and activities for the last sixteen years of his life.

Humphreys' interest in American production of fine woolen cloth may be traceable to Washington's dissatisfaction with the homespun inaugural suit he wore in 1789. His suit had been made from cloth produced in Hartford, at the first woolen mill built in the United States. Washington is said to have remarked that the cloth was "good but not yet of the best quality."[5] On 1 May 1792, Humphreys wrote to William Duer from Lisbon introducing a certain Mr. Douthal as "a Manufacturer from Ireland who proposes to settle in America. He is said to understand the woollen manufacture very well. I have told him America was a good place for those who understood the business, & would be industrious."[6] And in Spain Humphreys had observed the superior woolens produced from the fleece of the famous merino sheep. This wool was often combined with inferior sorts and even then produced some of the best cloth in Europe. When he left Spain in 1802, Humphreys requested a flock of one hundred merinos in place of the traditional gift given to departing ministers. The sheep were driven across Spain and Portugal and on 10 April 1802 were put aboard the *Perseverance* at Lisbon. The ship arrived at New York late in May with the loss of only nine sheep; the flock was then transported, by ship again, to Derby.

The year 1803 was relatively uneventful as Humphreys saw to the care and propagation of his flock. In March he was elected to the Connecticut Academy of Arts and Sciences. In October he sought state aid for the Society of Cincinnati in Connecticut and presented a "Memorial" to the legislature. Late in the year, after twelve months of renewing friendships and extensive traveling, Humphreys turned his attention exclusively to business. On 13 December he bought a saw mill, two fulling mills, and a clothier's shop at Rimmon Falls on the Naugatuck River. He enlarged the mills and arranged to receive cloth from private homes in the area in order to finish and prepare it for the market. Humphreys planned his operations with great care, proceeding slowly and cautiously.

The State Society of the Cincinnati dissolved formally at its annual meeting on 4 July 1804. Humphreys delivered the oration, *A Valedictory Discourse,* as it was called in its published form later that year.[7] The *Discourse* included a remembrance of the society's origins as well as a survey of America's political situation. Humphreys focused on his disapproval of the Louisiana Purchase, citing its unsuitability for settlement and agriculture as well as its cost as the foundation of his opposition.

A Valedictory Discourse is of particular interest because it contains the only known appearance of an untitled, 124-line antislavery poem.[8] Since *Miscellaneous Works* was registered by the clerk of the District of Massachusetts on 21 April 1804, and since the antislavery poem did not appear, it seems not to have been finished in time, placing its composition in late spring 1804. In its attachment to the principles of the Revolution, its recognition of the philosophical hypocrisy of allowing Negro slavery to exist in the United States, and its bold humanitarianism, the poem is worth special attention. Of particular interest is Humphreys' direct address to southern slaveholders, climaxing with a pointed denunciation of Jefferson:

And less shall plagues pursue those planter-lords,
    Who for proud wealth in slaves, their lot applaud;
Yet boast of liberty with guileful words,
    And preach "all men were equals made by GOD"?

Are ye the lords who treat your slaves as brutes?
    Heav'ns! how your deeds and doctrines disagree!
Speak not of freedom!—for your lip pollutes
    Your holy oath, "that man by birth is free."

Blush not these men, to government elect,
    Thy cause, Equality! who quaintly plead—
And talk of *declarations* that protect
    Man's natural rights—nor name that hateful deed

Themselves have done—to hold their blacks enthrall'd,
    To dole no daily food save stinted corn—
With whips to drive them, faint, with fetters gall'd—
    To tasks unending—and of hopes forlorn?

Say, then, perfidious!—say, are ye alone—
    Exclusive patriots?—Freedom's only friends?
Your eye-balls cas'd in scales, your hearts in stone
    On you the frenzying curse of Heav'n descends,

Ruin's forerunner! every act ye use
    To cheat the crowd with liberty's sweet name;
With hypocritic cant promote your views,
    Increase your slaves, and glory in your shame.

Speaking against the immorality of slavery, Humphreys was able to condemn the entire southern power group—and Jefferson most especially. At the same time, his own position was morally unassailable. He saw with perfect clarity the hypocrisy of those who even then continued to speak of the equality and freedom of all men but kept their own slaves all the while. He wrote, with the power of moral righteousness behind him, that one must demonstrate humanitarianism by deeds, not declarations. For those, like Jefferson,

who continued "to hold their blacks enthrall'd," Humphreys predicted the "frenzying curse of Heav'n."

To understand Humphreys' bitter criticism in the *Valedictory
Discourse,* one must see it within a biographical context. The poem
is an attack with many conscious and subconscious motivations. The
dissolution of the Society of the Cincinnati symbolized for Humphreys the end of an era. After Washington had died and his own
public career had ended prematurely, Humphreys viewed the passing
of the Cincinnati with more than sadness; the very spirit of the
Revolution appeared to be dead. Appropriately or not, Humphreys
identified Thomas Jefferson with all these misfortunes. Certainly
during the previous fifteen years Jefferson had come to be—for
Washington especially, though clearly for Humphreys as well—a
devastating political opponent. But Jefferson *was* vulnerable, and
the related subjects of slavery and hypocrisy presented an inviting
target. Humphreys could legitimately rail against Jefferson in a
poem with moral outrage—not personal invective—at its center.

Meanwhile, production in the woolen factory at Rimmon Falls
was necessarily slow. Humphreys occupied himself from 1804 to
1806 by watching over the growth of his flock of merinos, and he
saw, when he occasionally sold one, that their value had increased
steadily. In domestic matters Mrs. Humphreys found Boston agreeable, and during 1805, she and her husband looked for a parcel of
land upon which to build their new home. Early in February 1806,
they bought land on Oliva Street in Boston and built a large and
comfortable house. The new house was finished and occupied by 11
December 1807. During the last half of 1806, too, the frame for
the woolen factory had been raised and the mill had begun to mass-
produce wool cloth for the first time.

Late in 1806 Humphreys and his wife visited London, Paris, and
probably Lisbon, where they had been invited by old friends. While
in London, on 11 June 1807, Humphreys was admitted to the Royal
Society as a fellow. He was described as one "versed in several
Branches of natural knowledge," a man "likely to be an useful &
valuable Member."[9] At about the same time, Humphreys met John
Winterbotham, then a woolen manufacturer in Manchester. He
invited Winterbotham to be a junior partner in the Rimmon Falls

factory, in charge of the actual production of cloth. With the re-
cruitment of Winterbotham—as well as the gradual purchase of
land and equipment, the growth of the merino flock, and the steady
beginnings of the actual woolen production—the tentative first steps
had been taken and Humphreys' industry was ready for faster
growth.

Humphreys did very little writing after 1802. The muse apparently was less willing to inspire his pen while he was engaged in
the woolen industry than she had been while he was a soldier and
diplomat. But this should not be surprising. Humphreys' favorite
theme, after all, had been patriotism, and while he was in the public
service, patriotic poems were the appropriately sincere expressions
not only of his own love of country but that which he urged others
to feel as well. Humphreys could not view the domestic production
of wool in the same sublime, poetic terms as he had viewed the large
issues of war and peace. In addition, his recall from Spain seems to
have changed him. He could not have received the news with anything but regret at best—bitterness at worst. Then, too, his image
of himself as an altruistic public servant had been tarnished. Finally,
American taste for art was not very cultivated—or so Humphreys
seemed to feel. His sense of cultural superiority joined with his fall
from public service and his entry into the woolen industry to produce
a complex set of explanations for Humphreys' apparent disinterest
in literary matters.

One example of Humphreys' determined self-exile from the
American literary scene is contained in an 1806 letter to the Reverend Jedidiah Morse, who had apparently asked Humphreys to
undertake a critique of John Marshall's five-volume *Life of Washington*
(1804). Humphreys reminded Morse that he had already stated,
"in unusually strong language, . . . [his] reluctance in writing for
the public, (particularly in this country)." Furthermore, as his business interests increased, his "*inclination* and *leisure* for turning over
large volumes, have diminished, in somewhat the same proportion."
He continued: "With my sentiments of the national disposition
. . . the task in itself w'd be irksome. . . . The publick has no
claim to my literary Services—. . . . I prefer the bleatings of my
Merinos, with which I am surrounded to all the plaudits that could

be lavished by creatures, of [a] less innocent and [interesting?]
Species."[10] In November 1807, a year and a half after his letter to
Morse and after his European trip, Humphreys wrote to his kinsman,
Ozias Humphreys, in England: "On the subject of American literature & the state of the fine arts here, I can say nothing at present,
having had but little leisure & few opportunities, since my return
to make enquiries."[11] The truth seems to be that Humphreys had
fallen out of touch with developments in American literature by
1807, and this was apparently done by design: he had deliberately
abandoned literature.

Humphreys and his wife arrived home from their European trip
in September 1807. During the fall he wrote several interesting
letters, touching often on Anglo-American affairs. To Thomas Jefferson he wrote on 25 September that war with England seemed
imminent: "You may perhaps be surprised to learn that such independent Characters as your old friend John Stockdale, and many
others among the staunch friends of America in '76, look forward
to a war with us as an almost inevitable event not very much to be
deprecated, at least much less so than the loss of the smallest of
their naval rights."[12] On the same subject he wrote to Ozias Humphreys on 27 November, "if there be but one grain of common sense
in each of the Cabinets [i.e., American and British] there will be
no war."[13] Clearly, over the years Humphreys had maintained the
Federalist stance in foreign policy, even though the country—apart
from New England—was becoming politically unified under the
party line of Jeffersonian Republicans.

By late 1807 the woolen mill had survived the uncertain early
years and had grown into a successful operation. At that time,
Humphreys was able to say unequivocally that his effort to propagate
pure merinos in America had met with complete success. With the
propagation of the sheep and the impetus to produce homespun after
Jefferson's Embargo Act (December 1807), plus the added equipment, improved facilities, and expert management of John Winterbotham, the mill at Rimmon Falls began to produce more cloth
of higher quality than had ever before been produced in America.

The growth of the woolen mill into a successful business was
facilitated by one of Humphreys' proudest innovations in the de-

velopment of New England industrialism—the humanitarian employment of young people. Humphreys wrote to James Monroe in 1816: "If in any thing I have had an opportunity of being useful to my Country, perhaps I may indulge a consciousness of having been more so by setting an example of educating Youths at the Humphreysville Establishment, than in any other way."[14] In his "On the Necessity of State and Self-Defence" (22 June 1813), Humphreys commented on his sense of accomplishment regarding child labor: "I derive constant satisfaction from having given the first proof to the world that children may be employed and brought up in factories, without having their education neglected or their morals in danger of being corrupted."[15] Humphreys was, indeed, establishing a model for industrial communities in New England, caring for every facet of the boys' rearing—educational and moral.

Mrs. Ann Winterbotham Stephens, daughter of John Winterbotham, many years later recalled the employment of boys in the woolen mill:

Colonel Humphreys took great interest in the discipline and education of the apprentice boys attached to the factory. Seventy-three of these boys were indentured, I have been told, at the same time from the New York almshouse, and others from the neighboring villages. For these he established evening and Sunday-schools, with competent teachers; and indulged his military tastes by uniforming them at no light expense as a militia company, drilling them himself. Of course so many lads, gathered from the lower classes of a great city, must have numbered some bad ones. Thefts and other small vices were sometimes discovered, and at such times the offender was given his choice to be rendered up to the legal authorities, or tried and punished by a court organized on the premises. Almost invariably, they elected the latter, where they expected, and usually received a milder sentence than the severe laws of that period would have given.[16]

The testimony of another firsthand observer at Humphreysville, Timothy Dwight, further suggests the magnanimity of the enterprise: "In this manufactory he [Humphreys] has, I think, fairly established three points of great importance. One is that these manufactures can be carried on with success; another, that the workmen can be preserved in as good health as that enjoyed by any other class of men in the country; and the third, that the deterioration of morals

in such institutions, which is so often complained of, is not necessary, but incidental, not inherent in the institution itself, but the
fault of the proprietor."[17] Humphreys appears to have had ample
reason to be proud of instituting the prototype of industrial towns
in New England: his could boast of moral rectitude as well as
financial profit.

The final breach with England, resulting in a declaration of war
in June 1812, had been long anticipated by David Humphreys.
Political and international realities seemed to be urging him back
to public life; however, the public he chose to serve at that time
was in Connecticut only. At age sixty and as a veteran of the Revolution, Humphreys found himself during the War of 1812 in an
awkward position. His patriotism was intact, but his own political,
social, and financial allegiance was regional. Moreover, Connecticut
refused to supply the national government with troops. Still, Humphreys responded with his old military fervor and was commissioned
brigadier-general in the state militia. In addition, from 1813 to
1814 he served in the Connecticut state legislature. And, coinci-
dentally, while thus responding to the national and regional crisis,
he saw his woolen industry grow and prosper, for the embargoes
and protective tariff that followed promoted the rise of manufac-
turing in New England. Responding to his country's call had always
been a natural part of David Humphreys' character, one which he
could not entirely suppress, even though he disapproved of war with
England in 1812. By answering *Connecticut's* call, he believed he was
serving *America's* best interests. Clearly Humphreys faced a serious
moral dilemma regarding his own participation, a dilemma that was
complicated by his simultaneous business prosperity.

During the summer of 1812, Humphreys was soberly anticipating
the outbreak of hostilities. He wrote on 13 August to David Daggett, Connecticut's Federalist senator, expressing a guarded anxiety:
"A dumb & melancholly Silence prevails, like the awful Stillness
which precedes some tremendous phenomenon or destructive convulsion in the physical world.—I shall know more ere I leave 'this
Cradle of Liberty & Head Quarters of Good Principles.'—Much—
Every thing (perhaps)—depends on ourselves."[18] Not quite a year
later, on 22 June 1813, Humphreys delivered an address "On the

Necessity of State and Self-Defence" at the old meetinghouse on Academy Hill in Derby. The "Address," which prompted the organization of a statewide group known as "Veteran Volunteers," argues for the protection and preservation of Connecticut and its institutions. In a rush of patriotic language and sentiment, Humphreys called on the people of Connecticut, to defend their state, not the Union, although "in loyalty to the Union they yield to none." The people of Connecticut, he said, can "fulfil their constitutional obligations" by working for a speedy peace, and, in the meantime, they should join their neighbors in the state militia for the protection of themselves, their property, and their land.

Humphreys' military responsibilities were minimal during the War of 1812, although, as a man of position in Connecticut, his advice was sought and freely given. Throughout 1813 and 1814, he wrote regularly on the war, the bank, and the Hartford Convention to David Daggett in Washington. In a letter to Daggett dated 19 October 1814, he expressed his lack of confidence with the Madison administration: "I am almost rejoiced, that we are under such embarrassments in finances. It is from this cause alone, that you can hope for a termination of the war. We have no confidence in the Administration, or prospect of its speedy overthrow."[19] In the same letter he supported the forthcoming Hartford Convention: "You will have seen, or, at least, you will see by the time when you receive this, the Proceeding of old Massachusetts. They will have a good Delegation. The official Communication will probably reach our Executive tomorrow. We shall not be tardy in acting on the Subject, & co-operating with our Sister States in New England."

The Hartford Convention was convened on 15 December 1814 and met for three weeks, adjourning on 5 January with a list of seven constitutional amendments which were to be brought before Congress. While the convention was in session, the Peace of Ghent was signed (24 December), thus making the convention and its resolutions a gratuitous expression of America's disaffected New Englanders, who were trying, as they saw it, to regain their equal rights and benefits as sovereign states under the protection of the Constitution. The unfortunately timed convention and the Peace of

Ghent effectively destroyed the last vestiges of the Federalist party in the United States and put the final period to the story of David Humphreys' last foray into the area of public enterprise. With his eighteenth-century sense of responsibility for the public good and a concurrent dissatisfaction with the Republican policies of Jefferson and Madison, Humphreys offered himself to Connecticut and New England. He believed that by working for a peace he was providing the most sensible service to his country. Thus the prefactional patriot of the Revolution had found a way, perhaps the only way, to serve both country and region in the factionally divided War of 1812.

The Yankey in England

In January 1815 at Humphreysville, Humphreys' play, *The Yankey in England,* was acted out "by young persons, of both sexes, connected with the Institutions, in presence of clergymen, magistrates, selectmen, and other respectable citizens, with great applause."[20] By the time it was produced, Humphreys had the rare good fortune to have a widespread reputation as a "hero, a great gentleman, a public benefactor, and a man of letters."[21] *Yankey,* however, does not appear to have been solely the product of Humphreys' industrial days in Connecticut; it is almost certain, rather, that he had begun the work some twenty-two years earlier. He had written somewhat cryptically to Mrs. Nathaniel Greene in June 1792 from Lisbon about a comedy he had been writing: "The Comedy, if you will take my word for it, is an excellent one. At least there is the character of such a wife as I do not expect to come across in all my life; Though I have not put her in jeopardy of being burned, like my poor Widow of Malabar, I have put her (if possible) in a situation more interesting & affecting."[22] The comedy he mentioned in this 1792 letter grew sporadically into *The Yankey in England.*

If this dating is correct, the play takes an interesting place in the history of the Yankee as a character in early American drama. Even in 1792 Humphreys' "Yankey," Doolittle, would not have been a new character; he was modeled on Royal Tyler's Jonathan in *The Contrast* (1787). Certainly, however, the motivation for the play and some part of its composition was completed before Beach's *Jonathan*

Postfree; or, The Honest Yankey (1807) and Lindsley's *Love and Friend-ship; or, Yankee Notions* (1809). Even allowing for a later date than either of these, however, Humphreys' development of the Yankee as a character was the most significant step between Tyler's in 1787 and Mathews and Peake's *Jonathan in England* in 1824.[23] Hum-phreys' attempt to reproduce Doolittle's dialect faithfully accounts for the play's special interest. The eight-page glossary of American words and expressions appended to the play reveals Humphreys as an early and able student of the American language.[24]

The play in its published form is preceded, as was Humphreys' habit, by a number of prefatory materials—a letter, a note, a syn-opsis of the action, and of the greatest importance, "Sketches of American Characters." The "Sketches" generalize about the three-tiered social structure Humphreys observed in America. Those in the "first circles" of society, to use Humphreys' expression, are much the same in America as in England or elsewhere. Therefore, Amer-icans like General Stuart and Admiral Dixon in the play are indis-tinguishable from any English gentlemen. Humphreys also characterized the typical Americans, those not educated at the col-leges but who "had the advantage of what was called a grammar-school education." Mr. Newman in the play represented this class, which, in Humphreys' estimation, offered "respectable models for imitation." Humphreys, however, was insistent on distinguishing Newman from the typical Yankee—Doolittle, who, despite his poverty, had a public education sufficient to teach him "reading, writing, and keeping accounts." Humphreys' definition of the Yan-kee character deserves, by virtue of the uniqueness of the effort, closer attention. He wrote:

Although this Yankey, whose characteristicks in the abstract are designed to be personified in Doolittle, may be fairly a subject of risibility on account of his dialect, pronunciation, and manners; yet his good qualities . . . , doubtless, more than compensate for his singularities and failings.

Made up of contrarieties—simplicity and cunning; inquisitive from natural and excessive curiosity, confirmed by habit; credulous, from in-experience and want of knowledge of the world; believing himself to be perfectly acquainted with whatever he partially knows; tenacious of prej-udices; docile, when rightly managed; when otherwise treated, independent to obstinacy; easily betrayed into ridiculous mistakes; incapable of being overawed by external circumstances; suspicious, vigilant and quick of perception, he is ever ready to parry or repel the attacks of raillery, by retorts of rustic and sarcastic, if not of original and refined wit and humor.[25]

Humphreys' ear may well have been sensitive to the peculiar Yankee idiom and pronunciation after twelve years abroad. He drew Doolittle with careful attention to identifying details of speech and mannerism. He was able to see the Yankee character with uncommon perception, cutting through appearances to the reality beneath: simplicity, inquisitiveness, and credulity are mixed with suspiciousness, prejudice, and obstinacy to create a character of singular interest. These qualities, however, become believable only because of Doolittle's language—a language that the Connecticut audience had no trouble identifying. What other character type could be expected to say "keow" for "cow," "ort" for "ought," "sitch" for "such," "darter" for "daughter," or "despud" for "desperate"? In fact, the richness of Yankee expressions used by Doolittle is demonstrated in a glossary of nearly 300 terms identified and defined by Humphreys at the end of the play.

The play itself is notable only for Doolittle. The action is contrived, with all of the many interrelated missing persons reunited at the end of Act V. In addition to fathers, mothers, friends, and lovers being reunited, the hero's mother, long lost, is discovered to have been acting for many years as the heroine's surrogate mother. Finally, at play's end, the heroine receives all the inheritance that had been stolen from her. The happiest conceivable ending is worked out just a few hours before everyone is scheduled to sail for America.

On the way to this ending Doolittle mingles comically with all the characters, high and low. The humor he gives to scene after scene, however, is usually not of his own devising; the other characters and the audience are fully aware of his simplicity and credulity and are genuinely delighted by them. When, for example, Doolittle answers a knock at the Count's door, he is asked if the Count is at home. The Count replies aside to Doolittle that he is not at home, and Doolittle exclaims in a dither, "Not at hum! Not at hum! No; I spose I don't see him; but I vow, I du."[26] Still perplexed by the

Count's evasion, Doolittle later discusses it with the highly amused General Stuart:

Gen.   Oh, that is only an expression of the bon ton, in the beau-monde, to signify one is busy and cannot see company. That is nothing, nothing at all in this country.

Doo.   I don't know nothing about your *buns towns* and *bow moons,* in this country; but I'll be burnt alive if it would not be a lie with us in Varmount—and I always thought, till now, that a lie in one place was a lie every wheres.[27]

Occasionally, too, Doolittle's humor is sexual, as when the Count asks if he can keep a secret, and he replies, "I guess I du. And if you doubt it, you may ax the deacon's darter." Or, when General Stuart offers to make a man (i.e., a servant) of him, Doolittle replies, "A man of me! I'll tell the deacon's darter of that. She'll wonder what I was afore."[28]

Throughout, Humphreys portrayed Doolittle sympathetically, but from above. Doolittle's virtue stems from his Yankee simplicity, but Humphreys and the characters, who are of a higher class in the play, all laugh at him patronizingly. All would have agreed with General Stuart's relish at the thought of having conversation with Doolittle: "He looks like a true Yankey. If full-blooded, a conversation with him will be better than a scene in a comedy."[29]

Conclusion

Following the conclusion of the War of 1812, David Humphreys resumed his tranquil existence as the senior partner in T. Vose and Co., the official name given to his woolen industry. He continued to live in Boston, though he divided his time between Boston, New Haven, and Humphreysville. His interests remained wide, as his correspondence suggests. He wrote to David Daggett, for example, that the Bank of the United States (passed 10 April 1816) would "not equal the sanguine expectations of visionary Quacks in fiscal & political economy, by relieving us, at [once?] from all our pecuniary embarrassments."[30] Also in 1816, he published *A Discourse on the Agriculture of the State of Connecticut, and the Means of Making it More Beneficial to the State,* which concluded with the last poem

Humphreys wrote, "The Farmers' Harvest Hymn."[31] The poem is an uncomplicated thirty-six-line Thanksgiving hymn. Humphreys called on the farmers to thank the Lord of the harvests, and he prayed for peace so that Europe—by which he meant England—and America could "Unite their glorious toils." Clearly, he wished to see normal relations with England once again resumed.

In the last two years of his life, Humphreys' interests included a plan to use fumigation as a remedy against contagious disease. He also expressed concern for prison reform and the education of destitute children. Finally, during the summer of 1817, Humphreys became persuaded that a great sea serpent was, as contemporary reports had it, present at Gloucester, near Cape Ann. He went about collecting affidavits from those who had reportedly seen the monster, and from 2 September to 14 November he wrote a series of seven letters to Sir Joseph Banks, President of the Royal Society.[32] The entire series of letters is notable in its effort to maintain a proper scientific detachment. While of little importance historically or scientifically, Humphreys' report demonstrates still another turn of his mind, which responded in the eighteenth-century fashion to the greatest variety of natural, philosophical, literary, military, and political stimuli.

In a letter dated 9 February 1818 to Biglow and Holley—editors of the *American Journal* in New York—Humphreys inquired about the *Yankey*, which he had sent to them. In the same letter he referred passingly to a recent illness: "I have been extremely ill & absolutely confined within doors, by my increased cough & cold, ever since I came here [New Haven] from New York."[33] Although he felt a good deal improved by mid-February and apparently believed good health to be returning, David Humphreys died suddenly of heart failure on 21 February and was buried three days later at the Grove Street Cemetery in New Haven.

Despite David Humphreys' long and frequently distinguished career as a soldier, diplomat, businessman, and poet (one might reasonably add biographer, dramatist, and scientist as well), his death was not widely noted or long remembered. In fact, he was already an anachronism in 1818, a conservative figure of the American Enlightenment, who, for political reasons, had been left behind by national leaders. As a woolen manufacturer his successes were significant, though less satisfying to him because they were in the private sector rather than the public. Moreover, his patriotic verse was not as fashionable as it had been during the 1780s and 1790s, the years of his greatest popular success. In all, by 1818 his former renown as an officer of the Revolution, Federalist politico, competent diplomat, and patriotic poet had waned considerably. All who knew him during his last sixteen years continued to honor him for his past achievements and present business success, but it was clear that his was an unwanted Federalist voice from a bygone generation.

Humphreys' modest place in American literary, diplomatic, and business history has been secured by the extent of his interests and achievements—literary and otherwise—as well as his very excellent, eighteenth-century reputation. He was a distinguished American, a man whose many accomplishments have earned him a permanent place in the history of the nation.

Notes and References

Chapter One

1. Alexander Cowie, *Educational Problems at Yale in the Eighteenth Century* (Tercentenary Commission of the State of Connecticut, 1936), p. 11.

2. Quoted in Leon Howard, *The Connecticut Wits* (1943; rpt. n.p., 1969), p. 12.

3. Ota Thomas, "The Theory and Practice of Disputation at Yale, Harvard, and Dartmouth, from 1750 to 1800," Diss. State University of Iowa 1941, p. 17. Particularly helpful is Thomas's discussion of courses of study, pp. 90–102.

4. Thomas, pp. 95–96. Humphreys' role in this regard is also noted in William L. Kingsley, ed., *Yale College* (New York: Henry Holt, 1879), I, 95.

5. Frank Landon Humphreys, *Life and Times of David Humphreys* (1917; rpt. St. Claire Shores, Michigan, 1971), I, 29, and 31. Further references are identified as FLH, followed by volume and page numbers. See also Cowie, *Educational Problems,* pp. 27–28: "The aim of this society which was fathered by David Humphreys . . . was partly social; but it had a definite cultural object, which was to 'promote the intellectual improvement of its members by the study and practice of forensic debate, by the exercises in composition and elocution, and by the delivery at stated times of written orations and poems.' "

6. See John Ward, *A System of Oratory* (London, 1759), I, 307: *"Elegance* respects the purity, and clearness of the language. *Composition* regards the turn and harmony of the periods. And *Dignity* explains the nature and various kinds of tropes and figures."

7. Gordon E. Bigelow, *Rhetoric and American Poetry of the Early National Period* (Gainesville, 1960), pp. 16, 17, 24.

8. *The Miscellaneous Works of David Humphreys (1804),* "Introduction" by William K. Bottorff (Gainesville, 1968), p. 124.

9. Bigelow, pp. 48, 58. For the best discussion of the close relationship between epideictic oratory and poetry, see Theodore C. Burgess, "Epideictic Literature" in vol. 3 of *Studies in Classical Philology* (Chicago, 1902), pp. 89–261.

10. Bigelow, pp. 65, 67. See also Ward, II, Chapter XXXIV, "Of more Figures of Sentences, Suited to move the Passions."

11. "From there [Humphreys] wrote occasional verse letters to his predecessor, so playing a distant, minor part in the brief flurry of the New Haven renaissance. . . ." Howard, pp. 112–13. Alexander Cowie also makes some shadowy remarks about Humphreys' role in a "poetical correspondence" with John Trumbull. Cowie says that Humphreys "almost certainly" wrote what Trumbull termed a "very humorous [verse] letter in ridicule of Love, &c." *John Trumbull* (Chapel Hill, 1936), pp. 65–66. The most available complete text of this poem is in Edward M. Cifelli, "David Humphreys: The Life and Literary Career of an American Patriot with an Appendix of Previously Unpublished and Uncollected Poems," Diss. New York University 1977, pp. 265–68.

12. A long tradition places Humphreys at Philipse Manor from 1773 to 1776; however, only one scrap of corroborating evidence survives among the extant records of the Philipse family at the Sleepy Hollow Restoration Library at Tarrytown, New York. That evidence is in a letter from Frederick Philipse to his wife, dated from New Haven on 22 August 1776: "Just now heard that Mr Humphry's is made Adjutant of Militia at Darby and is Gone Down with the Regiment to New York who would thought it I am very positive that I should not have Credited it If a person of veracity had not Informed me of it[.]" Jacob Judd, "Frederick III of Westchester County: A Reluctant Loyalist," in Robert A. East and Jacob Judd, eds., *The Loyalist Americans* (Tarrytown, N.Y.: Sleepy Hollow Restorations, 1975), p. 43.

13. *Miscellaneous Works (1804),* p. 232. Unless otherwise noted, all quotations of Humphreys' poetry will be from this edition and will be identified as *MW.* Line references will be noted in the text, except where complete poems are quoted.

The most comprehensive statement on the sonnet in the last half of the eighteenth century in America comes from Mary Dexter Bates, "Columbia's Bards: A Study of American Verse from 1783 through 1799," Diss. Brown University 1954, pp. 291–92: "The sonnet, an almost forgotten lyrical form since Milton, its last great practitioner, was slowly regaining popularity. Charlotte Smith's *Elegiac Sonnets,* published in England in 1784, were reprinted in a new edition in Philadelphia in 1787. . . . Before the publication of *Elegiac Sonnets,* however, the sonnet had already been written in America. Bryan Edwards' *Poems, written chiefly in the West Indies* (Kingston [Jamaica], 1792) includes an Italian sonnet which he wrote in 1763. If David Humphreys' own dating can be trusted, the first of his twelve sonnets . . . was composed in 1776. . . ."

14. Julian Mason, "David Humphreys' Lost Ode to George Washington, 1776," *Quarterly Journal of the Library of Congress* 28 (1971):29–37. Mason's is the only known publication of the poem, long thought to have been destroyed.

The panegyric quality of much of Humphreys' work is traditional in epideictic literature: "Praise of a person enters into many forms of epideictic speech. . . . The odes of Pindar, besides supplying the prototype for the occasional address in general . . . , may easily have suggested the idea . . . of making an individual, his ancestry, deeds, virtues, and the myths suggested by the theme, the subject of a brief discourse." Burgess, p. 171.

15. ALS. Dated from Derby. New Haven Colony Historical Society.

16. Ward, I, 193.

Chapter Two

1. Casualties are listed in Mark Mayo Boatner, *Encyclopedia of the American Revolution* (New York: David McKay, 1966), p. 491.

2. From the *Life of General Putnam, MW*, pp. 304–305.

3. Letter quoted by FLH, I, 97–98.

4. *Life of Putnam, MW*, p. 319.

5. Letter quoted by FLH, I, 113.

6. *Life of Putnam, MW*, pp. 327–28. Boatner recalls Humphreys' version of Putnam's escape (p. 903), but says that he repeats it "not as history but as part of the American legend."

7. ALS. Dated New Haven, 10 April 1780. University of Michigan.

8. Ibid.

9. ALS. Yale University.

10. For similarities of language and image between the "Elegy" and Sonnet II, see Cifelli, pp. 38–39.

11. ALS. American Philosophical Society.

12. Humphreys revised the poem after 1780, probably in the summer of 1782, to include all the events and heroes of the Revolution; although it violates a chronological narrative, the following discussion is based on the revised text.

13. Both translations are by Dr. Charles Robinson, classicist from Morristown, N.J.

14. ALS. Humphreys to Jeremiah Wadsworth, 9 April 1781. Yale University.

15. Preface to "Address to the Armies," *MW*, p. 3.

16. Humphreys also wrote the following verse epitaph for Scammel, which he included in *MW*, p. 195:

Though no kind angel glanc'd aside the ball,
Nor fed'ral arms pour'd vengeance for his fall:
Brave Scammel's fame, to distant regions known,
Shall last beyond this monumental stone,
Which conqu'ring armies (from their toils return'd)
Rear'd to his glory, while his fate they mourn'd.

17. This appears to be the only contemporary verse account of Washington's spectacular success at Trenton. See Kenneth Silverman, *A Cultural History of the American Revolution* (New York, 1976), p. 404.

18. ALS. University of Michigan.

19. ALS. American Philosophical Society.

20. ALS. Dated from New Haven. University of Michigan.

21. See Boatner, p. 1047.

22. ALS. Connecticut State Library. The dating of the letter reads, "Head Quarters, near Passaic Falls 5th July 1780." The appointment carried with it a promotion to the rank of lieutenant colonel, which Congress belatedly formalized in the fall of 1782. From the time he joined Washington, however, until he died in 1818, he was known by most as Colonel Humphreys.

23. Many years later, in 1815, Humphreys had General Stuart reminisce in *The Yankey in England:* "I remember well, in the American war, the fate of Hale—of André. Victims too honourable! Not a dry eye in the American camp, when the latter suffered."

24. ALS. Dated 28 October. University of Michigan.

25. James Woodress, *A Yankee's Odyssey: The Life of Joel Barlow* (1958; rpt. New York, 1968), p. 59.

26. See note 18 above.

27. While the party was out, a rumor circulated that Humphreys had been captured. The rumor reached Ezra Stiles in New Haven, who made this entry in his diary for 5 January: "News that Major Humphry attempting to take Gen. Knyphausen is himself captivated at New York." *The Literary Diary of Ezra Stiles,* ed. Franklin Bowditch Dexter (New York: Charles Scribner's Sons, 1901), II, 491.

28. See note 14 above.

29. ALS. Dated "Head Quarters [New Windsor] March 31st 1781." Connecticut Historical Society.

30. See *The Writings of George Washington,* ed. John C. Fitzpatrick (Washington, D.C., 1931–44), XXIII, 299.

31. FLH (I, 234) quotes here the *Pennsylvania Gazette,* 7 November 1781.

32. Francis B. Heitman, *Historical Record of Officers of the Continental Army During the War of the Revolution* (Washington, D.C., 1914), p. 308.

33. One of the manuscripts is owned by the Connecticut Historical Society. It is part of an ALS, Humphreys to Wadsworth, dated "Head Quarters . . . April 24th 1782." The second is owned by the University of Michigan; it is signed but dated, vaguely, March 1782. The copy from the University of Michigan is printed here; however, where there are significant variations in the two versions, the variant will be noted in the text in brackets.

34. Ibid., ALS. Humphreys to Wadsworth.

35. According to Douglas Southal Freeman, the four months in Philadelphia "had been the most pleasant the General and his lady ever had shared. Formal dinners had been numerous. . . . Wherever the Commander-in-Chief appeared out of doors, crowds followed him. . . ." *George Washington* (New York: Scribner's, 1952), V, 403.

36. FLH, I, 252.

37. Letter dated from New Haven; quoted by FLH, I, 380. For a full discussion of the Huddy-Asgill Affair, see Katharine Mayo, *General Washington's Dilemma* (New York: Harcourt, 1938).

38. ALS. Humphreys to Greene. Dated "Head Quarters [?] Point Septr 24th 1782." Yale University.

39. The poem is unsigned but attributed to Humphreys by Charles Evans *(American Bibliography),* Charles Hildeburn *(A Century of Printing, . . . 1685–1784),* and Shipton-Mooney *(National Index of American Imprints through 1800).* In style and content the poem is very much like Humphreys's other work. The poem appears in its entirety in Cifelli, pp. 268–75.

40. See Freeman, V, 464 and 470.

41. Many years later, in "A Speech, Delivered before the Governor and Council . . . November 2, 1803" *(MW,* pp. 376–79), Humphreys commented with the same sentimentality on the disbanding of the army: "I remember well that day—nor can it be effaced from the memory of your Excellency. I have seen those veterans, (for, whatever their age, such they were after more than eight years service) without uttering one word, the tears secretly stealing from their eyes, grasping each others' hands at parting; and only consoled by the idea, I should rather say by the fond hope, that they might, perchance, meet on some future anniversary of independence. I must acknowledge my own feelings were never so much affected on any other occasion."

Chapter Three

1. ALS. Humphreys to Roger Sherman in Congress. Dated New Haven, 2 April 1784. Yale University.

2. Letter quoted by FLH, I, 292.

3. See Fitzpatrick, XXVII, 300–301.

4. Letter quoted by FLH, I, 302–303. From the beginning Jefferson was favorably impressed with Humphreys. In a letter to James Monroe of 21 May, Jefferson said that he had given Humphreys the first news of his appointment and that Humphreys "received real pleasure from it. He was before unknown to me; but our future connection in business has occasioned me to enquire into his character with which I am much pleased." Julian P. Boyd, et al, eds., *The Papers of Thomas Jefferson* (Princeton, 1950–), XVI, 59.

5. The letter to Franklin has turned up in two places. The original ALS is owned by the American Philosophical Society Library. This one is missing several key words. A copy of the letter in Humphreys' hand and with the key words intact is owned by the Bibliothèque Municipale in Nantes, France. For the letter to Jefferson, see Boyd, VII, 300–301. A copy of this letter, again in Humphreys' hand, is also owned by the Bibliothèque Municipale. The certificate is known only through the file copy found in Washington's Letter Book; see Boyd, VII, 301.

6. The text of the letter is taken from the ALS owned by the American Philosophical Society Library. Bracketed words and letters are supplied by the copy in the Bibliothèque Municipale.

7. The text of the letter is taken from the copy in the Bibliothèque Municipale, which differs in minor points of spelling and punctuation from the published version of the original as printed by Boyd, VII, 300–301.

8. In "Epistle from Dr. Dwight to Col. Humphreys" (dated Greenfield, 1785), Dwight replied with a somewhat more serious, patriotic poem. At the end, he implored Humphreys to return, "crown'd with every gift, and grace," ready "to add new glories to the western morn" *MW*, p. 221. (Poems in *MW* which do not have numbered lines are identified here by page numbers.)

9. ALS. Dated Paris, 9 November 1784. Historical Society of Pennsylvania.

10. Boyd, IX, 48–49.

11. Ibid., IX, 237.

12. Letter quoted by FLH, I, 341.

13. "Future Glory" is discussed in Chapter 5.

14. The major commentators on *The Anarchiad* agree that Humphreys supplied the idea for the work and that he borrowed it from *The Rolliad.* See, for example, Vernon Parrington, *The Connecticut Wits* (1926; rpt. New York, 1969), p. 428; William K. Bottorff, Introduction to Luther G. Riggs's edition of *The Anarchiad* (1861; rpt. Gainesville, 1967), p. x; and Leon Howard, p. 179. Howard's discussion of *The Anarchiad* is still the best available, pp. 169–205.

15. In order, these quotations may be found in Boyd, IX, 277; FLH, I, 345; Boyd, IX, 316–17; and Boyd, IX, 328.

16. The letter is quoted in Boyd, IX, 609. Boyd comments: "This appears to be the earliest recorded use of the word *Anti-federalist* as applied to one belonging to an identifiable political faction."

17. Ibid.

18. Letter quoted by Henry P. Johnston, *Yale and Her Honor Role in the American Revolution* (New York: G. P. Putnam's Sons, privately printed, 1888), p. 153.

19. Letters quoted by FLH, I, 307 and 318.

20. Ibid., I, 320–21.

21. Fitzpatrick, XXVIII, 202–204.

22. This interesting fragment is owned by the Rosenbach Foundation.

23. James Thomas Flexner, *George Washington: The Forge of Experience, 1732–1775* (Boston: Little, Brown, 1965), p. 24.

24. Letter quoted by FLH, I, 432.

25. This version is somewhat different from later versions; see Cifelli, pp. 275–76.

26. "Song" originally appeared as an untitled and unsigned poem. Humphreys later made a few minor revisions on it and reprinted it in *MW* (1804).

27. "The Genius of America" will be discussed later in this chapter as part of *The Anarchiad.*

28. Howard, p. 118.

29. "Humphreys' 'Ode to Laura': A Lost Satire," *Early American Literature Newsletter* 2 (1967):36.

30. Letters quoted by FLH, I, 364 and 375.

31. Letter quoted by FLH, I, 363.

32. 1 November 1786. Letter quoted by FLH, I, 373–374.

33. Fitzpatrick, XXIX, 27.

34. ALS. American Philosophical Society.

35. Letter quoted by FLH, I, 380.

36. Riggs, pp. 6–7. Further references are to this edition and are noted in the text.

37. Luther Riggs in the preface to his 1861 edition of *The Anarchiad* commented: " 'The Anarchiad' is universally conceded to have been written in concert by Humphreys, Barlow, Trumbull, and Hopkins; but what particular installment or number was written by either, has never been definitely ascertained. The fact that the papers were anonymously communicated to the publishers at New Haven, and that the authorship of any given portion of the work was never divulged by the members of this literary club, renders it almost impossible to fix upon any particular paper, or portion of a paper, and arrive at a certain knowledge in relation to its writer" (p. vi).

38. Letter quoted by FLH, I, 397.

39. Ibid., I, 390.

40. Ibid., I, 396.

41. Ibid., I, 401.

42. Harold C. Syrett, ed., *The Papers of Alexander Hamilton* (New York: Columbia University Press, 1961–69), IV, 241–42.

43. Letter quoted by FLH, I, 425.

44. ALS. Cornell University.

45. Thomas Philbrick, "The Sources of Cooper's Knowledge of Fort William Henry," *American Literature* 36 (May 1964):209–14.

46. Boyd, XIV, 304.

47. ALS. Mount Vernon, 7 April 1789. Historical Society of Pennsylvania.

48. Jared Sparks, ed., *The Writings of George Washington* (Boston: Russell, Shattuck, and Williams, 1836), X, 461.

49. Cf. Henry M. Wriston: "Washington desired that a chargé be sent rather than a minister. This was to be the first new diplomatic mission established by the new government; it involved a precedent. If a grade higher than chargé were to be sent to Lisbon, it might necessitate raising the level of the American missions to the more important countries—and thus the expenses of the diplomatic establishment would be greatly increased." *Executive Agents in American Foreign Relations* (Baltimore: The Johns Hopkins Press, 1929), pp. 316–17.

50. Jefferson to Humphreys, New York, 11 August 1790. See Boyd, XVII, 126.

51. Letter quoted by FLH, II, 26.

Chapter Four

1. 28 October 1790. Letter quoted by FLH, II, 50.

2. Ibid., II, 53.

3. Letter from Humphreys to Jefferson; dated from Lisbon on 30 November 1790. Quoted by FLH, II, 62–63.

4. Letter quoted by FLH, II, 65–66.

5. Ibid., II, 69–70.

6. *Poems* (Philadelphia, 1789), p. 49.

7. William G. Brooks, "Nathaniel Cutting's Journal of an Embassy to Algiers in 1793, Under Col. David Humphreys," *Historical Magazine* 4 (1860):262.

8. FLH claims (II, 149) to have published these lines for the first time. The fact is, though, that Humphreys himself published some of them in "Industry" (1794). Lines 399–411 and 427–36 were taken from the poem addressed to Mrs. Greene. The middle portion of the poem sent to Mrs. Greene, some twenty-nine lines in all, seem to have been published by FLH for the first time. The ALS, including the poem, is owned by the New Haven Historical Society.

9. Letter quoted by FLH, II, 142–43. More than two years after Humphreys mailed this letter, the poem was published by Mathew Carey (14 October 1794) as *A Poem on Industry—Addressed to the Citizens of the United States*. It was reprinted by Carey in 1796. The version of the poem appearing in *MW* (1804) is considerably different from the original and will be discussed separately in Chapter 5. Further references here are to the first Carey edition.

10. Letter quoted by FLH, II, 189–90.

11. 8 November 1794. Letter quoted by FLH, II, 226–27.

12. ALS. Dated Havre de Grace, 26 September 1795. Connecticut Historical Society.

13. The complete story of America's relationship with the Barbary states continued until Stephen Decatur led a naval force against them during the summer of 1815. The most complete version of this story, including Humphreys' key role during the intermediate period of the 1790s, is told by Ray W. Irwin, *The Diplomatic Relations of the United States with the Barbary Powers, 1776–1816* (1931; rpt. New York, 1970). See especially pp. 72, 82–84, 86, 88.

14. Copy of ALS provided by the William L. Clements Library.

15. 1 January 1797. Letter quoted by FLH, II, 253–54. The wedding occurred on 8 May 1797.

16. The preface is dated from the "City of Washington, in the Territory of Columbia, January 4th, 1803."

17. ALS. Dated from Lisbon, 27 April 1800. Rhode Island Historical Society.

18. Letter quoted by FLH, II, 254.

19. Humphreys quoted the letter in full in *MW* (1804), pp. 151–53.

20. Ward, I, 198.

21. It is impossible to date the sonnets with complete accuracy, although the evidence indicates that they are arranged in *MW* in the chronological order of composition.

22. To date the best discussion of the sonnets is Leon Howard's. He observed that most of them "represented a six-rhyme compromise between the Shakespearean and the Italian forms" (p. 259).

23. Letter quoted by FLH, II, 295.

24. Ibid., II, 336.

25. Edwin Cady comments on this resiliency of some Federalists: "Adherents of agrarian Federalism, the men like Noah Webster and Timothy Dwight who followed John Adams, seem to have had far less trouble surviving and adjusting to party defeat and changing times, bitter though they were. It was the silk-stocking Federalists, adherents of Hamilton, who gave way to reactionary despair." *The Gentleman in America* (Syracuse: Syracuse University Press, 1949), pp. 63–64.

Chapter Five

1. ALS. Dated 16 May 1800. Cornell University Library.

2. ALS. Madrid, 6 November 1801. Historical Society of Pennsylvania.

3. These all appear in *MW* (1804) under the following titles: "Remarks on the War between the United States and Tripoli" (New Haven, 1 November 1802); "Thoughts on the Necessity of Maintaining a Navy in the United States of America"; "Dissertation on the Breed of Spanish Sheep called Merino" (Boston, 25 August 1802); "Considerations on the Means of Improving the Public Defence: In a Letter to His Excellency Governor Trumbull" (Boston, 23 September 1803); "A Memorial of the Society of the Cincinnati in Connecticut" (October 1803); and "A Speech, Delivered before the Governor and Council, in support of the Preceding Memorial, November 2, 1803."

4. This and the following two passages are from *MW*, pp. 69, 82, 363.

5. FLH, II, 450.

6. ALS. Harvard University.

7. Published as *A Valedictory Discourse delivered before the Cincinnati of Connecticut in Hartford, July 4th, 1804, at the Dissolution of the Society* (Boston, 1804).

8. See Cifelli, p. 278. The poem is printed there for the first time since its original 1804 publication.

9. Certificate of Candidature. The Royal Society.

10. The quoted passages from this letter to Jedidiah Morse, dated 7 May 1806, are taken from a copy of the letter owned by Yale University.

11. ALS. Dated Boston, 27 November 1807. Harvard University.

12. Letter quoted by FLH, II, 362.

13. ALS. Harvard University.

14. ALS. Dated Boston, 16 May 1816. Yale University.

15. FLH, II, 393–94.

16. Mrs. Stephens's recollections were solicited for Orcutt and Beardsley's *History of the Old Town of Derby* (Springfield, Mass.: Press of Springfield Printing Company, 1880).

17. Barbara Miller Solomon, ed., Timothy Dwight's *Travels in New England and New York* (Cambridge, Mass.: Belknap Press of Harvard University Press, 1969), IV, 277.

18. ALS. Dated from Boston. Yale University.

19. ALS. Yale University.

20. *Yankey,* p. 111. All quotations from the play are to the 1815–16 publication of the work, a microfilm copy of which may be obtained from the Yale University Library.

21. Howard, p. 243.

22. ALS. Dated 20 June 1792. New Haven Colony Historical Society.

23. Walter J. Meserve, *An Outline History of American Drama* (Totowa, N.J.: Littlefield, Adams & Co., 1965), p. 68.

24. Cf. Howard, p. 265: Humphreys "failed to exact proper credit for the accuracy with which he represented [Doolittle's] dialect. After his long residence abroad Humphreys was unusually sensitive to 'Yankee peculiarities' in speech, and he apparently took particular care with them while revising his play for production. . . . Doolittle spoke a much more consistent dialect than had Jonathan in *The Contrast.* . . ."

25. *Yankey,* pp. 14–15.

26. Ibid., p. 54.

27. Ibid., p. 56.

28. Ibid., pp. 52, 79.

29. Ibid., p. 39.

30. ALS. Dated Boston, 6 April 1816. Yale University Library.

31. See Cifelli, p. 281 or FLH, II, 425–26.

32. *Letters from the Hon. David Humphreys, F{ellow} R{oyal} S{ociety} to the Rt. Hon. Sir Joseph Banks, President of the Royal Society, London; Containing*

Some account of the Serpent of the Ocean Frequently Seen in Gloucester Bay (New York, 1817).

33. ALS. New York State Library.

Selected Bibliography

PRIMARY SOURCES

1. Manuscript Material
Each of the following libraries and historical societies has given assistance in locating David Humphreys materials. In most cases these materials have been in the form of letters by Humphreys (identified as ALS, Autograph Letter Signed), but letters to him and about him, as well as his manuscripts and other related documents, have been supplied by the various libraries. The Library of Congress, the National Archives, and the Massachusetts Historical Society have provided information about the most accessible microfilm collections of their large Humphreys holdings.

It is a pleasure to acknowledge the helpfulness of library staffs throughout the United States and in France, England, and Spain as well. Many rare books were found at the very fine Washington's Headquarters Library at the Morristown National Historical Park. The New York Historical Society was similarly helpful. Special thanks go to the staffs at Yale's Beinecke Library and the New York Public Library's Rare Book Room. Finally, I am particularly grateful for the help of the late Paul Kinney, who, until the last months of his life, was reference librarian of the Sherman H. Masten Learning Resource Center at County College of Morris (Randolph, N. J.). Paul's patient and cheerful help was invaluable.

American Antiquarian Society: 3 ALS and several items of uncollected correspondence between DH and James Leander Cathcart.
American Philosophical Society Library: 8 ALS, 1 copy of a DH letter, and 2 letters about DH (from George Washington and Ezra Stiles, both to Benjamin Franklin).
Boston Public Library: 4 ALS.
British Library: 1 ALS.
Brown University Library: 2 ALS and 1 ms: "Elegy on Lieutenant de Hart" [n.d.].
Chicago Historical Society Library: 1 ALS.

Columbia University Library: 4 ALS, one copy of a DH letter, and 2 unsigned letters to DH.

Connecticut Historical Society Library: 155 ALS, 5 letters to DH, and 1 ms: "Adieu ye Scenes, so gaily formed to please" [titled elsewhere as "The Farewell"], 24 April 1782.

Connecticut State Library: 2 ALS.

Cornell University Library: 3 ALS and 1 letter to DH.

Dartmouth College (Baker Library): 2 ALS.

Duke University Library (William R. Perkins Library): 2 ALS.

Harvard University (William L. Lamont Library): 13 ALS.

Haverford College Library: 6 ALS.

Henry E. Huntington Library: 6 ALS, 1 copy of a DH letter, and 1 letter to DH.

Indiana University (Lilly Library): 1 ALS.

Library Company of Philadelphia: Rare edition of "The Glory of America; or, Peace Triumphant Over War," 1783.

Library of Congress: 4 ALS and 1 ms: "An Ode to his Excellency Gen'r¹ Washington," 1776.

Massachusetts Historical Society Library: Approximately 70 to 75 letters to, from, or about DH (the collection is scattered among the Knox, Pickering, and Heath papers).

University of Michigan (William L. Clements Library): 4 ALS, 1 letter to DH, and 1 ms: "The Farewell," March 1782.

Bibliothèque Municipale (Nantes, France): 2 copies of letters about DH (both written by George Washington and addressed to Benjamin Franklin and Thomas Jefferson).

New Haven Colony Historical Society: 5 ALS and DH's marriage certificate.

New York Public Library: 3 ALS.

New York State Library: 1 ALS.

University of North Carolina: 1 ALS.

Historical Society of Pennsylvania Library: 15 ALS, 1 copy of a letter by DH, and 1 ms: "Ode on Washington's birthday" [n.d.].

Princeton University Library: 2 ALS.

Rhode Island Historical Society Library: 3 ALS and 1 letter to DH.

Rosenbach Foundation: 1 ALS, 4 letters from Thomas Jefferson to DH, and 1 ms: untitled life of Washington [fragment], 1786.

The Royal Society: copy of DH's certificate of candidature.

Sleepy Hollow Restoration Library: extant records of the Philipse family.

Washington's Headquarters Library at the Morristown National Historical Park: Innumerable microfilms and rare books.

State Historical Society of Wisconsin Library: 3 ALS.

Yale University (The Beinecke Rare Book and Manuscript Library): 30 ALS, 1 unsigned letter, 1 copy of a DH letter, 1 letter about DH, and 2 letters to DH (one from Timothy Dwight and one from an unidentified printer).

2. David Humphreys' Works

Wherever possible the following list identifies the date of composition, first publication, important subsequent editions, and books of Humphreys in which the work is collected. The location of rarely reprinted poems is also noted. The works are listed chronologically.

Untitled and unsigned 8-line poem ["Immortal Pope!"], written 1770. Published 30 November 1770 in the *Connecticut Journal*. Reprinted in Cifelli, p. 265. (See below.) Attributed to Humphreys by Leon Howard, *Connecticut Wits,* p. 114.

"The Correspondent No. XXXII," written 1773. Published 23 July 1773 in the *Connecticut Journal*. 136-line verse letter, signed "H." Reprinted in Cifelli, pp. 265–68. (See below.) Attributed to Humphreys by Alexander Cowie, *John Trumbull,* pp. 77–78.

Sonnet I, "Adieu, thou Yale," probably written 1776. All 12 sonnets published for the first time in *MW* (1804).

"An Ode to His Excellency Gen'r¹ Washington," written 1776. First published in the *Quarterly Journal of the Library of Congress* 28 (1971).

"Elegy on the Burning of Fairfield," written March 1780. First published in the *New-Haven Gazette and Connecticut Magazine* (29 June 1786). Collected in *Poems* (1789), *MW* (1790), and *MW* (1804).

Sonnet II, "On the Revolutionary War in America," probably written early in 1780. Collected in *MW* (1804).

"Letter to a Young Lady in Boston" (also known as "Sleighing Adventures"), written in April 1780. First publication unknown. Collected in *Poems* (1789), *MW* (1790), and *MW* (1804).

"An Epitaph for Alexander Scammel," probably written shortly after Scammel's death in October 1781. First publication unknown. Collected in the *American Museum* (March 1788), *Poems* (1789), *MW* (1790), and *MW* (1804).

"Address to the Armies of the United States of America," written 1779–80; revised summer 1782. New Haven: T. & T. Green, 1780 and 1784. Also appeared in French translation by the Marquis de Chastellux. Paris: Perault, 1786. Collected in *Poems* (1789), *MW* (1790), and *MW* (1804).

"Elegy on Lieutenant de Hart," probably written 1780. First publication unknown. Collected in the *American Museum* (March 1788), *Poems* (1789), *MW* (1790), and *MW* (1804).

"The Farewell," written 1782. Published here for the first time.

"The Conduct of General Washington Respecting the Confinement of Captain Asgill placed in the True Point of Light," written 1782. Published in the *New-Haven Gazette and Connecticut Magazine* (16 November 1786).

Sonnet III, "On the Prospect of Peace, in 1783," probably written 1782. Collected in *MW* (1804).

"The Glory of America; or, Peace Triumphant over War," probably written summer 1782. Philadelphia: E. Oswald and D. Humphreys, 1783.

Sonnet IV, "On Disbanding the Army," probably written December 1783. Collected in *MW* (1804).

"An Epistle to Dr. Dwight," written summer 1784. First publication unknown. Collected in *MW* (1790) and *MW* (1804).

"Anacreontic" (also known as "Impromptu"), probably written in Europe, 1784–86. First published in the *American Museum* (March 1788). Collected in *Poems* (1789) and *MW* (1804).

"The Monkey Who Shaved Himself and His Friends," probably written in Europe, 1784–86; revised for first publication in the *Connecticut Courant* (26 February 1787). Collected in the *American Museum* (March 1788), *Poems* (1789), *MW* (1790), and *MW* (1804).

"An Epithalamium," probably written in England, 1785–86. First published in the *American Museum* (June 1787). Collected in *Poems* (1789), *MW* (1790), and *MW* (1804).

"A Poem on the Happiness of America: addressed to the Citizens of the United States," written in Europe, 1785. First published in London, 1786. Reprinted later that year in Hartford by Hudson and Goodwin. Also appeared in the *American Museum* (March 1787). Collected in *Poems* (1789), *MW* (1790). Revised for publication in *MW* (1804).

Biography of George Washington, written 1786. An unpublished fragment. Ms. owned by the Rosenbach Foundation.

"An Ode (Never before printed)." An early version of "An Ode Addressed to Laura." Probably written in 1786. First published on 6 July 1786 in the *New-Haven Gazette and Connecticut Magazine*. Reprinted in Cifelli, pp. 275–76. (See below.)

"An Ode Addressed to Laura," probably written 1786; revised for publication in the *American Museum* (March 1788). Collected in *Poems* (1789), *MW* (1790), and *MW* (1804).

"Song" (also known as "The Shepherd: A Song"), probably written 1787.
   First published on 20 September 1787 in the *New-Haven Gazette and
   Connecticut Magazine,* untitled and unsigned. Published in the *American
   Museum* (March 1788). Revised and collected in *Poems* (1789), *MW*
   (1790), and *MW* (1804).
"Mount-Vernon: An Ode," written summer 1786. First published in the
   Connecticut Courant on 9 October 1786. Collected in *Poems* (1789),
   MW (1790), and *MW* (1804).
The Anarchiad: A Poem on the Restoration of Chaos and Substantial Night. A
   collaboration of David Humphreys, John Trumbull, Joel Barlow, and
   Lemuel Hopkins. Collected and edited by Luther G. Riggs, 1861;
   facsimile edition, 1967. Twelve numbers, written from October 1786
   to September 1787, and published in the *New-Haven Gazette and
   Connecticut Magazine.* Individual numbers attributed to Humphreys:

   III.   28 December 1786
   IV.   11 January 1787
   V.   25 January 1787. This number was titled "The Genius of
          America: A Song." Collected in *Poems* (1789), *MW* (1790), and
          MW (1804).
   IX.   5 April 1787
   X.   24 May 1787

Sonnet V, "On Life," possibly written in fall 1787. Collected in *MW*
   (1804).
Sonnet VIII, "On the Immortality of the Soul," possibly written in fall
   1787. Collected in *MW* (1804).
The Widow of Malabar; or, The Tyranny of Custom: "imitated from the French
   of M. Le Mierre." Written 1788; produced May 1790. Published in
   MW (1790).
An Essay on the Life of the Honourable Major-General Israel Putnam. Written
   1788; presented to the annual Fourth of July meeting of the Connecticut Society of the Cincinnati, 1788. Hartford: Hudson and Goodwin, 1788. Collected in *MW* (1790) and *MW* (1804). Numerous
   editions available throughout late eighteenth and early nineteenth
   centuries.
Poems. Philadelphia. Mathew Carey, 1789. Thirteen poems, all previously
   published and all reproduced in *MW* (1804). *MW* (1790) contains
   all but "Anacreontic," also known as "Impromptu." Titles: "Fairfield," "Young Lady in Boston," "Address to the Armies," "de Hart,"
   "Monkey," "Laura," "Song," "Epithalamium," "Happiness of Amer-

ica," "Scammel," "Mount-Vernon," "Anacreontic," and "Genius of America."

"On the Political Situation of the United States of America," written 1789; delivered as an address to the Fourth of July celebration of the Connecticut Society of the Cincinnati, 1789. Collected in *MW* (1790) and *MW* (1804).

The Miscellaneous Works of Colonel Humphreys. New York: Hodge, Allen, and Campbell, 1790. Contains a prologue and epilogue to Racine's *Athaliah.* Date of composition unknown. Only known publication in *MW* (1790). Titles: "Address to the Armies," "Happiness of America," "Scammel," "Mount-Vernon," "Genius of America," "de Hart," "Monkey," "Laura," "Song," "Epithalamium," "Young Lady in Boston," "Epistle to Dr. Dwight," "Fairfield," *Widow of Malabar,* prologue and epilogue to *Athaliah, Essay on Putnam,* and "Political Situation—1789."

Untitled poem ["In thee, sweet Clime!"], written June 1792. 53-line poem, published in its entirety in Cifelli, pp. 276–77. (See below.) Ms. owned by the New Haven Historical Society.

"A Poem on Industry," written 1792. Philadelphia: Mathew Carey, 1794. Reprinted by Carey 1796. The poem underwent major revisions for *MW* (1804).

Sonnet VI, "On a Night-Storm at Sea," written 1795. Collected in *MW* (1804).

Sonnet VII, "On a calm Morning which succeeded a Night-Storm at Sea," written 1795. Collected in *MW* (1804).

Sonnet IX, "On the Death of Major John Pallsgrave Wyllys," possibly written 1795–97. Collected in *MW* (1804).

Sonnet X, "On the Murders committed by the Jacobin Faction in the early Period of the French Revolution," possibly written 1795–97. Collected in *MW* (1804).

Sonnet XI, "Addressed to his Royal Highness the Prince of Brazil, on my taking leave of the Court of Lisbon, July 1797." Collected in *MW* (1804).

"A Poem on the Love of Country," written 1799; delivered as a Fourth of July oration in Madrid. First published in *MW* (1804).

"Ode on Washington's birthday," written after 1799. 28-line poem. Published for the first time in Cifelli, pp. 277–78. (See below.)

Sonnet XII, "On receiving the News of the Death of General Washington," written 1800. Collected in *MW* (1804).

"A Poem on the Death of General Washington," written 1800; delivered as a Fourth of July oration in Madrid. First published in *MW* (1804).

Considerations on the Means of Improving the Militia for the Public Defence.
   Hartford: Hudson and Goodwin, 1803.
The Miscellaneous Works of David Humphreys. New York: T. and J. Swords,
   1804. Published or collected here for the first time:
   1.   All 12 sonnets, noted individually above.
   2.   "A Poem on the Future Glory of the United States of America";
        some 165 lines are added to the original conclusion of "Happiness
        of America" to form a new poem. The abridged "Happiness of
        America" is printed in *MW* (1804) for the first time.
   3.   "A Poem on the Love of Country," noted above.
   4.   "A Poem on the Death of General Washington," noted above.
   5.   "A Poem on the Industry of the United States of America"; 1796
        edition, revised. The original call to arms against Algiers is replaced
        with some 270 lines on Connecticut.
   6.   "Remarks on the War between the United States and Tripoli," 1
        November 1802.
   7.   "Thoughts on the Necessity of Maintaining a Navy in the United
        States of America," no date.
   8.   "Dissertation on the Breed of Spanish Sheep called Merino," 25
        August 1802.
   9.   "Considerations on the Means of Improving the Public Defence,"
        noted above.
   10. "A Memorial of the Society of the Cincinnati in Connecticut," Oc-
        tober 1803.
   11. "A Speech, Delivered before the Governor and Council, in support
        of the Preceding Memorial, November 2, 1803."
        Previously published and collected titles: "Address to the Armies,"
        "Happiness of America," "Fairfield," "de Hart," "Scammel," "Young
        Lady in Boston," "Epithalamium," "Anacreontic"—identified here
        as "Impromptu an Ode," "Epistle to Dr. Dwight," "Song"—iden-
        tified here as "A Pastoral from the French," "Mount-Vernon," "Ge-
        nius of America," "Monkey," "Prologue" and "Epilogue" to *Widow
        of Malabar, Essay on Putnam,* and "Political Situation—1789."
*A Valedictory Discourse delivered before the Cincinnati of Connecticut in Hartford,
   July 4th, 1804, at the Dissolution of the Society.* Boston: Gilbert and
   Dean, 1804. Includes a 124-line antislavery poem, untitled ["Heard
   ye a voice"]. Reprinted for the first time since 1804 in Cifelli, pp.
   278–81. (See below.)
"On a New Variety in the Breeds of Sheep," written 11 November 1811.
   Published in *Philosophical Transactions of the Royal Society* (1813).

"On the Necessity of State and Self-Defence; Gen. Humphreys' Address to the Inhabitants of Connecticut." Dated Humphreysville, June 22, 1813. Reprinted in FLH, II, 393–96.

The Yankey in England. Boston, 1815. Available on microfilm from the Yale University Library.

A Discourse on the Agriculture of the State of Connecticut, and the means of making it more beneficial to the State. Written 1816; published in New Haven: T. G. Woodward, 1818. Includes "The Farmers' Harvest Hymn." Reprinted in FLH, II, 425–26, and Cifelli, pp. 281–82. (See below.)

Letters from the Hon. David Humphreys, F{ellow} R{oyal} S{ociety} to the Rt. Hon. Sir Joseph Banks, President of the Royal Society, London; Containing Some account of the Serpent of the Ocean Frequently Seen in Gloucester Bay. New York: Kirk & Mercein, 1817.

SECONDARY SOURCES

Bates, Mary Dexter. "Columbia's Bards: A Study of American Verse from 1783 through 1799." Diss. Brown University 1954. Discussion of early American sonnets. DH's contribution may be measured within this context.

Beers, Henry A. *The Connecticut Wits.* New Haven: Yale University Press, 1920. An interesting, early treatment of the Wits.

Bigelow, Gordon E. *Rhetoric and American Poetry of the Early National Period.* University of Florida Monographs, Humanities no. 4. Gainesville: University of Florida Press, 1960. Traces the methods and ideas linking the arts of poetry, oratory, and persuasion. Indispensable if one is to understand the epideictic traditions out of which DH's poetry arose.

Bottorff, William K. "Introduction" to *The Miscellaneous Works of David Humphreys* (1804). Gainesville: Scholars' Facsimiles & Reprints, 1968. Makes most of DH's work available.

———. "Introduction" to *The Anarchiad: A New England Poem* (1786–1787). Edited in 1861 by Luther G. Riggs. Gainesville: Scholars' Facsimiles & Reprints, 1967. The 12 numbers of *The Anarchiad* were never collected until the Riggs edition in 1861; the facsimile edition makes the work available.

———. "Humphreys' 'Ode to Laura': A Lost Satire." *Early American Literature Newsletter* 2 (1967): ii. Claims the ode is a successful *"vers de societé."*

Boyd, Julian P., et al., eds. *The Papers of Thomas Jefferson.* Vols 1–19.
    Princeton: Princeton University Press, 1950–74. Scattered through-
    out is a great deal of Humphreys' correspondence.

Burgess, Theodore Chalon. "Epideictic Literature." Reprint from vol. 3
    of *Studies in Classical Philology.* Chicago: The University of Chicago
    Press, 1902. Like Bigelow, this, too, is indispensable if one is to
    understand the kinship between epideictic oratory and poetry.

Butterfield, Lyman H., et al., eds. *Adams Family Correspondence.* 2 vols.
    Cambridge, Mass.: Belknap Press of Harvard University Press, 1963.
    Some helpful correspondence to and about Humphreys.

Cifelli, Edward M. "David Humphreys: The Life and Literary Career of
    an American Patriot." Diss. New York University 1977. Contains an
    appendix of previously unpublished and uncollected poems,
    plus an extensive bibliography.

Coe, Edward B. "The Literary Societies." In William L. Kingsley, ed.,
    Yale College: A Sketch of its History. 2 vols. New York: Henry Holt
    and Company, 1879, pp. 307–24. Discusses DH's participation in
    the Brothers in Unity.

Cowie, Alexander. *John Trumbull: Connecticut Wit.* Chapel Hill: The Uni-
    versity of North Carolina Press, 1936. A good study of another Wit;
    touches occasionally on DH.

Fellows, John. *The Veil Removed; or Reflections on David Humphreys' Essay on
    the Life of Israel Putnam.* New York: James D. Lockwood, 1843. Proves
    that DH was a mythmaker, not a historian.

Fitzpatrick, John C., ed. *The Writings of George Washington.* 39 vols. Wash-
    ington, D.C.: The United States Printing Office, 1931–44. Contains
    important correspondence to DH.

Heitman, Francis B. *Historical Record of Officers of the Continental Army
    During the War of the Revolution.* Washington, D.C.: The Rare Book
    Shop Publishing Company, 1914. Handy account of DH's war service.

Howard, Leon. *The Connecticut Wits.* 1943; rpt. Ann Arbor: University
    Microfilms (authorized Xerographic reprint), 1969. See especially
    Chapter IV, "David Humphreys" and Chapter VIII, "The Honorable
    David Humphreys." The best discussion of DH as a writer.

Humphreys, Frank Landon. *Life and Times of David Humphreys: Soldier-
    Statesman-Poet, "Belov'd of Washington."* 2 vols. 1917; rpt. St. Clair
    Shores, Michigan: Scholarly Press, 1971. The most comprehensive
    study of DH in his various careers. Very little about DH as a writer,
    however.

Irwin, Ray W. *The Diplomatic Relations of the United States with the Barbary Powers, 1776–1816.* Definitive account of DH's role in the freeing of the Algerine captives.

Jaffe, Irma B. *John Trumbull; Patriotic Artist of the American Revolution.* Boston: New York Graphic Society, 1975. Interesting account of a man whose life and work paralleled DH's.

Marble, Annie Russell. *Heralds of American Literature: A Group of Patriot Writers of the Revolutionary and National Periods.* Chicago: University of Chicago Press, 1907. Maintains that DH's "besetting sin [was] literary vanity."

————. "David Humphreys: His Service to American Freedom and Industry." *New England Magazine,* N.S. 29 (1904):690–704. "Few men of his age contributed such efficient services to American freedom in such diverse ways."

Martin, John Stephen. "Social and Intellectual Patterns in the Thought of Cadwallader Colden, Benjamin Thompson (Count Rumsford), Thomas Cooper, Fisher Ames, Timothy Dwight, David Humphreys, Benjamin Silliman, and Charles Brockden Brown." See Chapter VII, "David Humphreys and the Delayed Vocation of a 'Natural Aristocrat.'" DH's "delayed vocation" was the woolen industry.

Mason, Julian. "David Humphreys' Lost Ode to George Washington, 1776." *Quarterly Journal of the Library of Congress* 28 (1971):29–37. Makes this early poem available for the first time.

Parrington, Vernon L. "Introduction" to *The Connecticut Wits.* 1926; rpt. New York: Apollo-Crowell, 1969. Important for its generally sympathetic remarks as well as for making the work available.

Philbrick, Thomas. "The Source of Cooper's Knowledge of Fort William Henry." *American Literature* 36 (1964):209–14. Cooper's debt to DH.

Silverman, Kenneth. *A Cultural History of the American Revolution.* New York: Thomas Y. Crowell Company, 1976. A fine history that touches DH's work several times. Especially good commentary on "Happiness of America."

————. *Timothy Dwight.* New York; Twayne Publishers, 1969. Important study of another Wit; touches occasionally on DH.

Thomas, Ota. "The Theory and Practice of Disputation at Yale, Harvard, and Dartmouth, from 1750 to 1800." Diss. Iowa State University 1941. Shows the growing importance of rhetoric and English forensics at Yale when DH was a student.

Woodress, James. *A Yankee's Odyssey: The Life of Joel Barlow.* 1958; rpt. New York: Greenwood Press, 1968. This study also touches on DH occasionally.

Index